The Phenomenon
that was *Minder*

The Phenomenon that was *Minder*

by Brian Hawkins

Inkstone
Books

THE PHENOMENON THAT WAS *MINDER*
© 2002 Brian Hawkins
ISBN 962-86812-1-4

Typeset in Centaur by Alan Sargent
Cover design by PPC Ltd, http://www.powerpointcreative.com
Printed in the United Kingdom

Acknowledgements

Photographs of Glynn Edwards (page 20) and Nicholas Day (page 46) kindly provided by the artists, photograph of George Cole (page 63) by the author. The author gratefully acknowledges the following for permission to use their copyright images:
DC Thomson & Co. Ltd (front cover and pages 12, Dennis Waterman and 16, George Cole); Curtis Brown (page 18, Gary Webster), Jo Ryan (page 24, Patrick Malahide).

Minder © 1979–2002 Thames Television Ltd (a FremantleMedia company). Copyright of the *Minder* television programme and its characters is protected by Pearson Television. The concept of the *Minder* television programme was created by Leon Griffiths and the programme was produced by Euston Films Ltd for Thames Television Ltd.

*Inkstone Books (a division of Chameleon Press) http://inkstone.chameleonpress.com
23rd Floor, 245–251 Hennessy Road, Hong Kong*

Contents

Preface

I first saw *Minder* in 1981 when I lived in Western Australia. I can remember that my first reaction was that the programme was a little odd. It was billed as a follow-up to *The Sweeney*, but apart from the fact that it starred Dennis Waterman there seemed to be little similarity. However, it was set in London and took me back to a time when I was growing up in London surrounded by people using cockney rhyming slang. I have always been fascinated by the cockney argot, and this fascination was further strengthened after I did an anthropological linguistics unit at the University of Western Australia and found myself spending more time listening to how people sounded than what they actually said. But at that time in Australia I only caught a few episodes of the first season of *Minder*.

A couple of years later I was living in Hong Kong and *Minder* used to go out in the television dead spot of the day — Sunday lunchtime — complete with Chinese subtitles (a story in themselves). There was always something else to do at that time and I started to build up a collection of home-recorded videotapes of the programme to watch later. By chance, I also happened to acquire a number of off-air videos of the show made by my friend, Terry Dean, in Australia. Another friend, at the University of Hong Kong, David Workman, had also collected a number of videotapes and it was his casual remark, 'Between us we've probably got enough tapes to write a book' that was the genesis of this one. I did a little research and discovered that there was no reference book available on the series. I decided then to write one.

Over many years, and particularly with the help of the Internet, I tracked down and watched every episode. I am grateful to everyone who has provided me with videotapes. My brother John in England kindly sent me his tapes of the final season and the elusive first episode of the eighth season in which Gary Webster played Ray Daley for the first time.

Every episode synopsis in the book is mine. Other people will no doubt watch the programme and identify a different set of salient points. If readers wish to contact me to point out what they see as deficiencies or errors in the synopses I would be pleased to hear from them.

The key word list is also very subjective. What one person sees as a key word another person might gloss over as trivial. I welcome suggestions from readers on anything they feel is worthy of listing (addressed care of Inkstone Books, or by e-mail to brian@minderphenomenon.com).

The cast lists presented something of a problem. The intention was to list all the performing artists, regardless of their level of participation. But not all of the videotapes to which I had access had complete programme credits. I therefore spent several days at the British Library Newspaper Library in Mill Hill, North London, copying the *TV Times* programme listings for every episode of *Minder*. The listings were also not always complete and for space reasons would occasionally omit some of the minor characters. Also there were occasional discrepancies between the spelling of names in the programme credits and the spelling in *TV Times*. In that case the programme credit was regarded as authoritative. The *TV Times* cast listings were originally in order of appearance, but this seemed to vary in later years. The listings in the programme credits appear to be loosely in order of importance of the character. Some artists have appeared in the series at different times using different spellings for their names (e.g. Pete Postlethwaite and Peter Postlethwaite). In the alphabetical list in this book these artists are listed under separate names. The lists are therefore as complete and accurate as I was able to make them. If there are any errors or omissions I would be pleased to hear about them.

For the writers and directors, the information given in this book is exactly as listed in the programme credits. Where an individual has worked on two or more episodes under different names (eg David Yallop and David A. Yallop; Dave Humphries and David Humphries) the individual is listed in this book under separate names exactly as in the programme credits.

I am grateful to Nury Vittachi in Hong Kong for introducing me to Peter Gordon of Chameleon Press, who was a mountain of support. Alan Sargent in Hong Kong worked wonders with the layout and provided invaluable technical advice in the production of this book. I also thank my wife Janice for much of the early typing of the manuscript and for her help in laboriously transcribing information at the British Library Newspaper Library. Stuart

Hawkins read through several drafts of the manuscript and made many valuable suggestions.

Lastly, I wish to record my gratitude to cast members George Cole, Glynn Edwards, Patrick Malahide, and Nicholas Day for their generosity and patience in providing information and material for use in this book. There is no doubt that their involvement has resulted in a far better product than might otherwise have been.

BRIAN HAWKINS
HONG KONG
OCTOBER 2002

A phenomenon in the making

Prelude to a phenomenon

Autumn 1979 was not a glorious time in Great Britain. Unemployment and inflation were reaching record levels. Public morale was low. The new Conservative government under Mrs Margaret Thatcher had recently unveiled a highly unpopular budget. The country was still reeling from the effects of months of industrial strikes that had brought down the Labour government and led to the 'Winter of Discontent'. One such industrial dispute at London's Thames Television came to an end on 24 October after blacking out the entire Independent Television network for close to 11 weeks.

Against this dismal background, Thames Television introduced its new action series for the autumn season on Monday 29 October — a programme with the intriguing title *Minder*. The show was already weeks overdue, the new season's line-up traditionally being unveiled in early to mid-September.

At that time, nobody could possibly have imagined the eventual success that *Minder* would enjoy. Today, probably due in large part to the series, the term 'minder' is generally understood to mean a bodyguard or assistant. In 1979, this usage was much less familiar, and the idea that such a relationship could sustain a television series for over 100 episodes would have seemed highly improbable. But by the time the programme ended in 1994 it could account for ten seasons, 104 52-minute episodes, a 60-minute Christmas special, a Christmas compilation of excerpts, two feature films and two different actors playing the minder. The programme became a major hit not only on British television but was also sold to over 70 countries around the world, making it one of Britain's top TV exports. At the peak of its success, in 1985, nearly 18 million people a week in Britain were watching the show.

But in Autumn 1979, *Minder* was unashamedly intended as a vehicle for its leading actor, Dennis Waterman, to capitalise on his popularity in an earlier Thames Television series *The Sweeney*, that had recently come to an end.

Dennis Waterman (Terry McCann)

Dennis Waterman

Dennis Waterman was no newcomer to acting and came with excellent credentials. Born in London on 24 February 1947, he attended the Corona Stage School. He made his debut at the age of 11 in the 1958 feature film *Night Train to Inverness* and later appeared in the West End production of *The Music Man*. In 1962 he was cast in the title role of BBC television's 13-part series *William* based on the stories of Richmal Crompton.

The Sweeney, in which Waterman co-starred with John Thaw, was a no-holds-barred action series based in London about two officers in Scotland Yard's Flying Squad (known as the 'Sweeney Todd' in rhyming slang). Dennis Waterman played the part of Detective Sergeant George Carter while John

Thaw played Carter's guv'nor, Detective Inspector Jack Regan. In its quest to achieve gritty realism, the programme's action sequences, tough dialogue, car chases and violence — on both sides of the law — set a new standard in British police shows. There were regular complaints from the police about its portrayal of police brutality but the public could not get enough of the programme or its two stars.

When *The Sweeney* finished its run in 1978, its production company began to look for another role for Dennis Waterman. The company, Euston Films, had been set up six years earlier as a subsidiary of Thames Television specialising in film production, and was headed by George Taylor and Lloyd Shirley. Before *The Sweeney* its major output had been the 1972 series *Special Branch* starring George Sewell and Patrick Mower, and a six-part series under the general title *Armchair Cinema*. One of these episodes, *Regan*, written by Ian Kennedy Martin and directed by Tom Clegg, was the pilot of *The Sweeney*.

The successor to *The Sweeney* came in the form of a film script called *Minder* penned two years earlier by veteran television writer Leon Griffiths about an East End crime boss and his bodyguard.

As Terry McCann in *Minder*, Waterman played a young man with two prison terms under his belt, one for grievous bodily harm and the other for attempted robbery. At least one of these was for a crime that his boss was involved in but escaped prosecution. At one time McCann had had a career ahead of him as a professional boxer but he lost his licence after a rigged bout in which he took a fall that was too obvious. According to his boss, Arthur Daley, he should have been nicked for overacting.

The character he took on in *Minder*, as the tough, streetwise yet slightly naïve underdog had many similarities to his role as Sergeant Carter in *The Sweeney*, the sidekick of the powerful Inspector Regan.

Leon Griffiths

Born in Sheffield in 1928, Leon Griffiths (named after Leon Trotsky by his staunchly communist mother) had a tough upbringing in Glasgow where he developed a hankering to be a writer. After leaving school he obtained a job as an assistant director in a small film company. He left the company to perform his National Service and found himself working with the British Forces Network in Germany alongside fledgling broadcaster Cliff Michelmore. By the time he had completed his National Service the film company he worked for previously had gone bankrupt. To pay the bills he took up a writing post with the *Daily Worker* in the 1950s and eventually became their drama critic. He relinquished this position, and indeed his communist ties, following the invasion of Budapest by Russian tanks in 1956 and struggled to make a career on Fleet Street.

Griffiths got into television script-writing almost by accident following a chance offer to write some episodes of the independently produced *The Adventures of Robin Hood* series from 1955–59 starring Richard Greene. Griffiths was not the only one out of the political mainstream to work on the *Robin Hood* series. Executive producer Hannah Weinstein also used the talents of several blacklisted US writers (usually working under pseudonyms) who had taken refuge from Senator Joseph McCarthy's notorious communist witch-hunt back home.

In script-writing, Griffiths found a vocation and branched out into writing television plays and film scripts, often in the crime thriller genre and incorporating the undercurrent of dark humour, incisive wit and cleverly crafted dialogue that became his forte.

He wrote prolifically for television, ranging from the 1959–60 ITV series *Four Just Men,* based on the stories by Edgar Wallace, to Yorkshire Television's 1979–80 series *The Racing Game* based on the stories of Dick Francis. He was at home in the sleazy aspects of his plots, from horse-race fixing in *The Racing Game* to his 1978 BBC-1 *Play for Today* entitled *Dinner at the Sporting Club* involving rigged boxing contests — a theme that was to reappear a few years later in a *Minder* episode. Coincidentally, in the 1978 story, it was John Thaw from *The Sweeney* who gave an exceptional performance as the boxing manager who suffers the indignity of seeing his prize boxer forced to lose a fight.

Among Griffiths' notable film credits was *The Grissom Gang* in 1971 based on his earlier play *No Orchids for Miss Blandish,* in which a kidnapped socialite falls in love with one of her abductors. In *The Grissom Gang* he took an essentially violent plot and interspersed a sprinkling of humour — an approach that he also adopted later with the early episodes of *Minder.*

In an interview with *TV Times* in 1991, Leon Griffiths described how he used to go to afternoon drinking clubs in North London and meet people who gave him ideas for his characters, including Arthur Daley in *Minder:* 'I've always been fascinated by low life, the semi-villains of this world. I like observing them, wondering how they make out.' He went on: 'They lived on their wits and were great storytellers. I don't suppose half of what they said was true but it didn't matter. They were alive; they crackled with a sort of crazy energy."

Griffiths' original conception of *Minder* was as a tough, hard-hitting gangland film which he had kept on hold for a couple of years on the advice of his agent who felt that it was a little too serious to sell at that particular time. The same agent later suggested that Griffiths rework the film into a television script using two of the characters from the film: a small-time crook with a second-hand car business and his streetwise bodyguard (or 'minder', as the term was in East London).

When Euston Films saw the revised script they immediately recognised it as an ideal vehicle for Dennis Waterman to play the part of the minder, an ex-boxer with a prison record. When Waterman saw the initial scripts and story lines he was particularly taken by the underlying humour and needed no second thoughts about accepting the part.

The task then fell to producers George Taylor and Lloyd Shirley at Euston Films to cast the supporting role of Arthur Daley, the smooth-talking used-car salesman, always on the lookout for a quick quid. The script called for someone 'the same age as some good-looking American film star [Arthur Daley often announced proudly that he was the same age as Paul Newman]. He's totally behind the Home Secretary as far as law and order is concerned. His favourite film is *The Godfather* and he dresses like a dodgy member of the Citizens' Advice Bureau.' A number of artists were considered but the final choice went to television and film veteran George Cole.

George Cole

George Cole was no stranger to the Arthur Daley character he took on in *Minder*. In a career spanning over 40 years, he had already made a name for himself in the 1950s and '60s as the smooth-talking spiv Flash Harry in the highly popular St Trinian's comedy films about a girls' boarding school.

Born in London on 22 April 1925, Cole made his stage debut at the age of 14 in the 1939 West End production of *White Horse Inn*. The following year he was cast as a young wartime evacuee in the movie *Cottage to Let* starring the legendary comedy character actor Alastair Sim.

George Cole (Arthur Daley)

Alastair Sim became a tremendous influence on young George Cole's career. Cole recalls: 'The toughest task Alastair and his wife Naomi had was trying to get rid of my cockney accent. It was very strong but they succeeded. Luckily, I was able to reclaim it for *Minder.*' Their technique, he described, was to get him to stand up and tell jokes and then cover their ears with their hands when he got to the punch line. Mild perhaps, but apparently effective.

Sim and Cole worked together on two of the St Trinian's films (*The Belles of St Trinian's* in 1953 and *Blue Murder at St Trinian's* in 1958) and in several other films and stage productions. Cole also appeared without Sim in *Pure Hell at St Trinian's* in 1961. The early St Trinian's films are clearly dear to Cole's heart, as they are to most people who had the good fortune to enjoy them as family entertainment when they were first released. He now talks with genuine sadness about the salacious direction the concept took with the 1980 release of *The Wildcats of St Trinian's* (in which he did not appear).

A number of stage and screen roles followed for Cole after St Trinian's, usually in the light comedy genre in which he seemed to fit naturally. He also had a long spell in the popular *A Life of Bliss* series on BBC radio and then in the same series on television, but it was *Minder* that propelled him to the pinnacle of his profession.

George Cole's Arthur Daley character was a successful middle-aged businessman who owned a second-hand car business and a lockup in Fulham filled with a motley collection of assorted items that had fallen off the backs of countless lorries over his questionable career. He had had some minor skirmishes with the law in the past but now managed to keep his activities one step ahead of the police. There are occasional references to him having served time in prison more than 20 years ago, but he writes it off as 'just a bit of petty'.

Easily mistaken for a bookie with his fat cigar, trilby hat and expensive overcoat, Arthur Edward Daley was the quintessential small man made good. He mostly drove a Jaguar but, being in the car business, also drove other luxury cars from time to time including a Daimler, a Mercedes, and a Rolls-Royce, depending on what came his way. Creator Leon Griffiths actually wrote the Jaguar into the original script. He said: 'Arthur could only ever have driven a Jaguar. It has always been the kind of car the people he admired aspired to.'[2]

Daley had two children in private schools, lived in White City, and was in awe of his wife, who was never seen in the series, to whom he referred — almost reverently — as "er indoors'. He deluded himself into believing he was a pillar of society. There are even occasional hints that he is a Freemason but this is not specified.

We never hear in the series exactly where and how Arthur Daley and Terry McCann first met. The opening title sequence of the first seven seasons showed Arthur meeting Terry on his release from prison and trying to interest him in a Ford Capri on the car lot (in reality a location near Brook Green in London W14). Although we see the pair shaking hands on the deal, we never know whether Terry paid for the car or whether it was provided as some form of compensation, or even a bribe to win back Terry's loyalty. We do learn as the series unfolds that Terry's flat is provided by Arthur and that Terry pays

Gary Webster (Ray Daley)

him rent. He did not receive a regular wage from Arthur but occasionally took a small cut of whatever Arthur made by hiring him out. Although Terry always played second fiddle to Arthur, the show set out as a vehicle for Dennis Waterman, and it was Waterman's name that appeared first in the credits.

After 70 episodes, seven seasons and two feature films, Dennis Waterman quit the series, and his Terry McCann character was written out by having him emigrate to Australia.

Gary Webster

Following the departure of his first minder, Arthur Daley was forced to take on a replacement. Reluctantly at first, he took on his nephew, Ray Daley, played by Gary Webster. Although with some stage work to his credit,

26-year-old Webster was a relative newcomer to television, his major experience playing the character Graham in ten episodes of BBC-1's *EastEnders*.

Ray Daley was very different from Terry McCann. Unlike Terry, who had received limited formal education but was streetwise and handy with his fists, Ray Daley was educated. He had 'O' levels in French and woodwork. He knew how to handle himself when the going got tough but preferred to talk his way out of trouble. He was teetotal, unlike Terry who was an avowed lager drinker. Gary Webster continued to play Ray Daley for three seasons until the show came to an end in 1994.

Glynn Edwards

The other stalwart of the show was Dave Harris (played by Glynn Edwards) who was always there in the background throughout the series as the unflappable, benevolent manager and barman of the Winchester Club. This was a fictitious private drinking club based on one in Chalk Farm that was frequented by Leon Griffiths and used as the location for the Winchester Club in the first few episodes. Here, Arthur Daley would make his plans, arrange his business meetings, and invariably end up downing a vodka and tonic when his shady business deals went awry. Although it was a legitimate drinking club, the Winchester Club was also a magnet for petty criminals. Arthur fitted in well there.

Dave was the soul of discretion and had a generous share of common sense. Arthur, on the other hand, though impulsive, had business acumen, an entrepreneurial spirit and the smooth patter of an East London market man. As an ex-schoolmate, lifelong friend and counsel of Arthur's, Dave was the perfect buffer to exert some moderation over Arthur's questionable activities.

In one of the later episodes in the series, *Gone with the Winchester*, we see the relationship between Arthur and Dave nearly torn apart when one of their boyhood friends visits the club on his release from a long prison spell and starts putting divisive ideas into Arthur's head. But Arthur finally learns the value of friendship, and the relationship is restored. Glynn Edwards recalls this as one of his favourite episodes: 'It was a part I could really get into and develop the character. For me it was a nice acting experience. But if you ask me which episode was the most fun, it would have to be the one where we

Glynn Edwards (Dave Harris)

all went off to Calais for the day with Arthur to buy some cheap booze. That was a lot of fun.'

Glynn Edwards, who appeared in 94 of the programme's 108 episodes, could not have been a better choice for the role. Trained at Joan Littlewood's Theatre Workshop, he appeared in over 20 feature films including *Zulu* in 1964 and *Get Carter* in 1971 (in which he came to a painful end at the hands of Michael Caine). He had countless television appearances to his credit spanning an acting career of more than 25 years and he brought impeccable professionalism and credibility to the role of Dave. But it was a role that he nearly passed over. He recalls: 'When it came up it was just another job. An idea of a series was the last thing on our minds. I was offered a day's work playing a barman. In fact, I nearly turned it down as it was such a small job. But my agent pushed me and said it was worth doing in case it led to something bigger. And then they called me back for another episode and the part really took off. It finished up as probably the most important job in my career.'

Without a doubt, Dave became a firm favourite with the viewing audience. Glynn Edwards believes that one reason for Dave's popularity was that Arthur's wife was never seen in the series. 'Dave was a sympathetic soul,' he pointed out, 'and a good listener. In a way Dave somehow took the place of Arthur's wife as someone to listen to his problems. He was a sort of confidante of Arthur's and I think the audience needed that.'

Glynn Edwards was born on 2 February 1931 in Penang in what was then Malaya where his father was in the rubber industry. He had a variety of jobs before embarking on his acting career including working on a sugar plantation in Trinidad. At one time he was married to the late Yootha Joyce who played Mildred in the popular television series *George and Mildred.*

Season 1   29 October 1979–21 January 1980

Publicity for *Minder*'s debut on British television in 1979 was sadly lacking, due in no small way to the industrial dispute that had shut down the whole Independent Television network and delayed the scheduled commencement of the series. To make matters worse, the *TV Times* was also affected by an industrial dispute and only a skeleton version was being printed. This prevented the hype and promotion that would normally accompany the start of a new series. The *TV Times* listing for the first episode described it simply as 'a new series starring Dennis Waterman as Terry (the Minder) and George Cole as Arthur (his guv'nor)'. No other cast were listed. The following week the programme was listed as *The Minder,* 'a thriller series starring Dennis Waterman as Terry, an ex-convict who must tackle a variety of difficult and dangerous bodyguard assignments arranged by his smooth boss'. Again, there was no cast list, episode title or other information. From the third week the programme was fully listed with cast, episode title, synopsis and major technical credits.

Gunfight at the OK Laundrette

The first episode, *Gunfight at the OK Laundrette* by Leon Griffiths, went out in the 9–10 p.m. time slot on Monday 29 October 1979. The opening credit sequence, which remained almost untouched for seven seasons (apart from slightly tighter editing and some new shots at the start of the second season), saw Terry McCann driving into Arthur's car lot in a Ford Capri (SLE 71R) with Arthur in the passenger seat. We then see a series of black and white stills interspersed with the film to explain how Terry came to be there: he is outside a prison gate; checking under the bonnet of the Ford Capri; the winner of a boxing match; shaking hands with Arthur on the car deal; and finally out on the town with Arthur in the West End.

Gunfight, with singer and entertainer Dave King co-starring in a straight role, could easily have filled a conventional drama slot. The story was based on a real-life siege at a pizza shop in Knightsbridge. While acting as a temporary bodyguard for Alfie, the character played by King, Terry accompanies Alfie to empty the coin machines at his laundrette business and walks straight into an armed hold-up. The robbers, who claim they are members of a black militant group, take Terry, Alfie and an elderly woman customer as hostages. Terry manages to defuse the situation but, with his criminal record for violence, is suspected of being an accomplice. Although he emerges as the hero, Terry suffers the indignity of being forced to lie face-down in the road while the police search him at the end of the siege. Arthur was there watching from behind the police barricades, wearing the fawn overcoat that became his trademark. The humour, which added little to the story line, came from Arthur's attempts to exploit the situation by selling the story to the press.

When the episode was repeated 14 years later, after the series had come to an end, Max Davidson in *The Daily Telegraph* described it as 'uncannily prophetic'. He wrote: 'The way Terry was presumed guilty by the police on the basis of his previous form — despite being, on this occasion, the hero of a siege in a laundrette — anticipated a theme which has dominated police dramas since the Guildford Four and Birmingham Six cases.'[1]

The episode began a tradition that extended over the programme's entire run of using a title that was a parody or pun of a well-known film title, book title, song title, popular expression, etc. *Gunfight at the OK Laundrette* obviously referred to the 1957 film *Gunfight at the O.K. Corral.* Typical of the titles that followed were *Minder on the Orient Express* (after *Murder on the Orient Express*), *The Dessert Song* (a clever pun on *The Desert Song* for an episode involving dubious catering supplies), *Monday Night Fever* (after *Saturday Night Fever*), and *The Birdman of Wormwood Scrubs* (about a newly released prisoner who kept a cage bird while he was in prison, after *The Birdman of Alcatraz*).

Lloyd Shirley and George Taylor, who had worked together on *The Sweeney*, produced the first episode along with executive producer Verity Lambert, and the three remained as the senior production team for the first three seasons.

The first episode was directed by Peter Sasdy, who directed two other episodes in the first season. Tom Clegg, a highly respected TV director who had been with Euston Films for years, was originally invited to direct the first two episodes but turned it down because he didn't like the story. Other directing stalwarts who worked on the first season included Roy Ward Baker, Francis Megahy and Ian Toynton.

George Cole recalled how he and director Peter Sasdy were instrumental in establishing an important part of Arthur Daley's characterisation. He explained: 'Peter had decided that he wanted Arthur to be a smart dresser, so he sent me off to Savile Row to buy two suits. But the producers were far from pleased when I got back and told them the suits cost £400 each. That wasn't in the budget! A bit later on we were shooting a scene in which I was supposed to grab one of the characters and start a fight. I said to the director, "We can't do that. Do you know how much this suit cost? If we so much as make a mark on it the producers will go mad." The director said, "Well what are we going to do then?" I thought for a while and said, "How about, when I see him, I duck around the corner and let Terry sort it out?" And from then on, whenever there was a fight scene, Arthur ran the other way!'

Patrick Malahide

The first episode saw Patrick Malahide in the first of 24 appearances as the droll, bumbling Detective Sergeant Albert 'Charlie' Chisholm, always determined to get Arthur 'bang to rights'.

Malahide recalls: 'For the first episode I was paid for just half a day to turn up to play this copper, and would I bring my own suit? In those early episodes you can still spot me with long hair and a trendy seventies whistle. From then on if they needed a copper they would call me. It wasn't until the

Patrick Malahide (DS Chisholm)

second or maybe even the third series that they told me I was a regular. It was only then that I was allowed to really focus the character the way I wanted and the designer and I went out and bought this awful brown suit and a porkpie hat.'

An identity crisis

The first few episodes, with varying amounts of humour, served to establish the characterisations, but suffered from a definite identity crisis. Was it comedy? Or was it drama? The *TV Times* had promised 'a thriller series', but a thriller, in the conventional sense, it was not. The problem was not helped by Dennis Waterman's continued public identification as Sergeant Carter from *The Sweeney*.

One of the most important elements that contributed to the success of *Minder*, but added to the classification dilemma, was that it was made on film. At that time, editing of videotape was still notoriously time-consuming and expensive. Television drama was almost invariably made on videotape: in a studio with three or four cameras covering the same scene, extensive rehearsal, and with the director assembling the shots as they were being performed.

Recording on film provided considerably more flexibility than tape. Film cameras at that time were more manoeuvrable than conventional television cameras. A single film camera was usually all that was required for a shot. Film cameras could get into spaces that television cameras could not and allowed comprehensive and relatively inexpensive editing of the recorded material. But most importantly, film allowed the material to be shot on location, something that was technically difficult using videotape.

Minder was originally conceived to take over where *The Sweeney* left off. *The Sweeney* had been shot on film and much of its success had been achieved from its rich use of London locations and its fast-paced action sequences that would have been impossible in a studio. And so it was that in *Minder* we see extensive and imaginative use of locations. Indeed, the entire programme was shot on location: derelict factories, allotments alongside railway tracks, car repair shops under railway arches. There was an element of realism and credibility that would be hard to reconstruct in a studio.

On top of this there was the comic dialogue. This was confusing. British comedies were generally made in a studio in front of a live audience and with canned laughter added afterwards confirming that we were supposed to laugh. In *Minder*, the cues to the viewing audience were somehow missing. This also placed additional demands on the actors. They had to adjust their delivery to allow the audience time to laugh and not miss the line that followed. On top of all this, *Minder* was perceived as a follow-up to *The Sweeney* — a programme notoriously short on humour. It was no wonder the audience was confused.

Beyond the siege

With only four cast members credited apart from Waterman and Cole, the second episode, *Bury My Half at Waltham Green* by Paul Wheeler, looked as if it had been made on a shoestring budget. The episode saw Terry minding a bank robber (played by *Randall and Hopkirk [Deceased]* star Kenneth Cope) on his release from prison. Unlike the previous episode, in which the humour was peripheral, the humour in this episode was central to the story line: a decoy prisoner, a clumsy minder and the payoff at the end. There was a mild car chase and only a hint of violence, but we were introduced to another facet of Terry's lifestyle when we saw him in bed with a woman he had just met, the wife of the mastermind behind a bank robbery who was still in prison. The producers were apparently still working on the characterisations and we heard Arthur Daley speaking with a cultured accent that was very unlike the accent we heard for the rest of the series.

The third episode, *The Smaller They Are* by Leon Griffiths, saw the introduction of violence as an integral part of the story line. The episode dealt with a small-time bag snatcher played by Phil McCall who unknowingly crosses a gang of international currency smugglers. The episode reintroduced Glynn Edwards as Dave, the manager of the Winchester Club. We also met Peter Childs for the first time as Rycott, the other member of the local plod with an interest in putting Arthur away. In this episode he is still a detective constable after 15 years on the force following some unspecified 'trouble' earlier on. In later episodes we see him as a detective sergeant.

'Er indoors

The third episode saw the first reference to Arthur's unseen wife as "er indoors'. When Arthur and Terry see an attractive young girl at the bar of a pub Arthur says, 'See, that's what 'er indoors don't understand. A young bird like that hanging round keeps yer feeling young.' Terry replies, 'I thought it was Phyllosan and Grecian 2000.' Phyllosan was a proprietary vitamin tonic tablet aimed at the over-forties, and Grecian 2000 a hair dye.

The term "er indoors' soon found its way into the vernacular and became an established way of referring to a spouse (replacing *'er* with *'im* where appropriate). The term was also the basis for a Christmas novelty record in 1983 written by Dennis Waterman. *What Are We Gonna Get 'Er Indoors?* (backed with *Quids and Quavers*) featured Cole and Waterman in their Arthur and Terry characters and spent five weeks in the UK pop record charts. The record reached number 21 in the charts and even merited an appearance of the duo on the BBC's flagship *Top of the Pops* music show.

Writer and creator of the series, Leon Griffiths, later said that he first heard the term used by a London minicab driver.[1] The driver could have achieved some degree of fame for coining the expression except that when Griffiths saw the man a second time he denied ever saying it.

It was probably the same taxi-driver described by John Hurry Armstrong in Griffiths' obituary in *The Independent*.[4] According to this version, the taxi-driver was a drinking companion of Griffiths and always used the term to describe his wife who was never seen with him in the pub. The story has it that Griffiths was terrified that his friend would be upset when the term was first used in the series. As it turned out, the taxi-driver was not at all concerned, firmly believing that all husbands called their wives 'er indoors and never took them to the pub.

Arthur referred to his wife as 'er indoors in virtually every episode that followed. But she was never seen and we never even got to hear her name. (In Leon Griffiths' novel *Minder*,[5] published as a tie-in three months before the programme first went to air, Arthur Daley's wife was called Sarah.) Dave at the Winchester Club would use 'er indoors to refer to her, or occasionally the more formal Mrs Daley. In later episodes, Arthur's nephew Ray would refer to her as Auntie.

We never saw her but we felt that we knew her well. A simple, 'She's got these feet' from Arthur was enough to elicit a whole story and make us realise that we've all met someone just like her at some time or another. Little hints were dropped from week to week until we had built up a mental profile of her: she doesn't actually play the piano, 'she likes polishing things' . . . 'I must get home, 'er indoors is doing fish' . . . 'Don't keep on, you're beginning to sound like 'er indoors. There you go again, that's 'er to a T' . . . 'I promised to take her shopping at Brent's Cross. She'll go potty if I don't turn up.' But she had good taste: ''er indoors has been agging me for a couple of nice chairs to go with the Regency stripe we've had bunged up on the lounge wall.'

''Er indoors' was immortalised by the *Oxford English Dictionary* in 1997:

> **her indoors** (also **'er indoors**) *Brit. colloq.*, one's wife or girlfriend; in extended use, applied to any woman occupying a position of authority who is regarded as domineering. The phrase was popularized by the Thames Television series *Minder* (1979–93) in which the leading character Arthur Daley habitually referred to his wife as 'her indoors'.

The dictionary attributes the original usage of the term to L. Griffiths in 1979 in the second draft of the script of *The Smaller They Are*. Leon is probably chuckling in his grave at the knowledge that he inspired an entry in the *OED*.

The identity crisis continues

The fourth episode, *A Tethered Goat* by Murray Smith, did nothing to help the viewer decide whether the series was comedy or serious drama. In this episode, Terry minds an Arab banker who is being pursued by some Middle-Eastern hit men. Some scenes could have come straight out of one of the tough police dramas that had gone before such as *The Sweeney* and *The Professionals*. There is plenty of action, cars driven at high speed, hit men jumping through glass windows, realistic fights, guns and graphic violence — even Arthur Daley takes a punch. Alongside the heavy drama was a hilarious performance by Kenneth Griffith as Dai Llewellyn, the Welsh manservant whom Arthur has conjured up to attend on the Arab.

Episode 5, *The Bounty Hunter* by Bernie Cooper and Francis Megahy, saw comedy provided by George Layton in the first of his six appearances as Des, a crooked motor mechanic, and serious drama by classical actor Derek Jacobi as the mastermind behind a Majorcan property scam.

An undercurrent of violence or implied violence continued throughout the remaining six episodes of the first season but the show seemed to become more sure of where it was going and the audience had come to appreciate the balance between drama and humour. The last episode in the season, *You Gotta Have Friends* by Leon Griffiths, ended with Arthur being forced to jog around Hampstead Heath by actor George Baker playing a health fanatic who has threatened to kill Arthur unless Terry can recover £70,000 he believes Arthur has stolen. The sight of Arthur Daley, bemoaning 'I'm a goner' after his enforced jog and being helped along by Terry was a classic blend of comedy and pathos.

The season's ratings were far from excellent — but sufficient for executive producer Verity Lambert to persuade Brian 'Ginger' Cowgill, programme controller of Thames Television, to fund another season.

Season 2   *11 September–18 December 1980*

By the second season, beginning on 11 September 1980, Leon Griffiths, who had written six of the 11 episodes in the first season, had suffered a severe stroke that left him with a speech impediment and unable to write. But with typical humour he remarked that he was too weak to write a suicide note, let alone another *Minder* script.[6] Nonetheless his resilience and willpower showed through and he responded to an intense regime of physiotherapy and speech therapy over the next couple of years.

Prominent among the new writers brought in by Linda Agran, script executive at Euston Films, following Griffiths' illness was Tony Hoare. He had already written one of the episodes from the first season (*Come in T-64, Your Time is Ticking Away*) and had writing credits for several crime shows including *Z Cars*, *Softly Softly* and *The Bill*. As a former bank robber who started writing while serving a prison sentence in the 1960s, he was an ideal choice for *Minder*. In 1994, he told the *TV Times* that he sometimes felt that he *was* Arthur Daley: 'I've done bird, I've lived down the East End and have a lot of pals who are villains.' To get ideas for the show, he said, 'I just stand in an East End pub listening to all the stories.'[7]

The new writers came up with a broad range of ideas in the second season. We saw Terry minding a racehorse in the first episode and a prize bull in the last, a boxer in one and a wayward footballer in another. The racehorse episode, *National Pelmet* by Willis Hall, made it into the top 20 of the ratings charts and the programme's popularity began to grow.

The story lines managed to touch on a number of contemporary social issues. *Not a Bad Lad, Dad*, by Tony Hoare, was one of the most sensitive episodes in the entire run of the series. This dealt with marital violence, and saw the appearance of a nine-year-old boy on Terry's doorstep with a note from the child's mother claiming that he was Terry's son from a brief affair. *All Mod Cons*, by Andrew Payne, also dealt with a pressing social issue, this time in the form of homelessness and the exploitation of the homeless by heartless landlords. In this episode we see Toyah Willcox as a ruthless landlady charging rent to a young couple for a slum dwelling and then trying to evict them as squatters.

Caught in the Act, Fact, by Tony Hoare, originally intended as the final episode in the season, sees Terry receive a suspended prison sentence for shop theft after he minds a female magistrate with kleptomania. Despite being in a position to clarify the matter and prove Terry's innocence, Arthur is more interested in saving his own neck. This episode elicits genuine sympathy for Terry's naïvety, and contempt for Arthur's manipulation of him. It would have made an ideal close to the season. The audience was with Terry all the way when he turned his back on Arthur at the end of the episode to go his own way. The effect was sadly diluted when, due to a programming quirk, they appeared together again the following week enticing a bull into a truck.

Looking back at these early episodes there are some noticeable differences from present-day television drama. Political correctness, for example, was something quite new and was clearly not of major concern to the script-writers. A reference to 'dopey spades' (i.e. blacks) had to be edited out before the first episode could be shown again 14 years later. In another of the early episodes (Episode 5) there is a throwaway line in which we see Terry speaking to an Indian car cleaner in a Peter Sellers-type, mock Indian accent, that would be regarded as highly offensive today.

In Leon Griffiths' *In* in the third season, Arthur is threatened with a charge under the Race Relations Act for racially insulting a German police inspector. He replies, 'That's for Lucozades, not Jerries' (i.e. spades not Germans). In other episodes, we hear blacks referred to as *lemonades* (more rhyming slang on *spades*) and *schwarzers*. In Tony Hoare's *Whose Wife is it, Anyway*, Terry is minding an antique shop that has been the subject of demands for protection money. An overt homosexual played by Alun Lewis runs the shop. In this episode we hear the gay character referred to as 'a raving iron', 'a poofter', 'a queen', and 'a woofter'. In the same episode we see Terry in bed with the shop owner's wife while her husband is in hospital recovering from a hit and run accident.

Sexual permissiveness in television drama was regarded very differently during the show's early years from the way it was when the series ended in 1994. During the first three seasons we see Terry in bed with several different women, including rock singer Suzi Quatro in *Dead Men Do Tell Tales*. Arthur Daley summed him up in that episode: 'The boy's obsessed with crumpet. I think he's after the Queen's Award for Industry — and it drains his strength.' But all this came to an abrupt end on the direct instructions of senior management when the dangers of AIDS and HIV transmission started to become known.

The depiction of violence was also handled differently in those early days. One of the most violent episodes, *The Old School Tie* by Jeremy Burnham, saw both Dave and Debbie, Terry's girlfriend, receive severe beatings by thugs, the smashing up of Arthur's lockup, and Terry taking on a group of thugs in an elaborately-staged fight in a car-breaker's yard. The incidents were in context and added to the realism, but raise doubts about how acceptable they would be in today's climate of sensitivity to violence. Gratuitous and even contextual violence were significantly pruned by the company around the time of the third season to comply with the new broadcasting standards instituted in response to demands by public morals campaigner Mrs Mary Whitehouse and her supporters.

Ratings during the second season remained good but not outstanding and it was probably thanks to a Writers' Guild award to Leon Griffiths in 1980 (despite his not having written any episodes for the second season) that Thames Television agreed to a third season.

In an unexpected spin-off that either contributed to the show's popularity or resulted from it, the theme tune became a successful single record. *I Could Be So Good For You* (backed with *Nothing At All*), co-written by Dennis Waterman and Gerard Kenny and sung by Waterman, reached number three in the UK charts in November 1980. The song reached number one in both the Australian and the New Zealand charts and in 1981 received an Ivor Novello award for 'The Best Theme from TV and Radio'.

The Christmas season of 1980 also saw the publication of the first *Minder* annual, an 'authorised edition', meaning that it had received the blessing and support of Thames Television. The front cover consisted of a large photograph of Dennis Waterman. Indeed, the majority of the text centred heavily on Waterman and his Terry character, with George Cole's Arthur Daley clearly relegated to a supporting role that left no doubt as to the perception of the show from a management point of view.

Season 3   13 January–7 April 1982

After a year's break from the screen following the second season, the third season began in January 1982. Suddenly, the programme's popularity began to rocket. The season opened with a hilarious episode *Dead Men Do Tell Tales*, by Tony Hoare, featuring three highly respected comedy artists Patricia

Maynard (Waterman's wife at the time), Harry Fowler and Derek Fowlds, and singer Suzy Quatro as Terry's grass-smoking girlfriend. In this episode Arthur has to keep a coffin containing a body in his lockup and Terry later has to drive around London with the coffin on the roof rack of his car. In view of the sensitive nature of the story line, the episode was preceded by a warning to viewers. Comedian Mike Reid appeared the following week in Andrew Payne's highly amusing episode *You Need Hands* as a minder with a taste for fine food and wine. This episode dealt with illicit drugs and was also preceded by a warning to viewers.

The third episode, *Rembrandt Doesn't Live Here Anymore* by Dave Humphries, saw George Sewell as an ex-forger with a talent for copying valuable paintings, not as fakes but 'in the style of' the original. One, of a racehorse, particularly captivated Arthur: 'It's so good it makes you want to reach out and give it a sugar lump'. Clever one-liners abound and show that comedy for comedy's sake was now an essential part of the programme's ethos. Arthur, on Morocco: 'That's full of Arabs ennit — standing round in their night-shirts getting dysentery.'

The programme seemed to have found the direction it was heading and the third season was played mainly for laughs, utilising guest artists of the calibre of Max Wall, Avril Angers, Gareth Hunt, Alfie Bass, Michael Medwin, George Sewell, Richard Griffiths and Nigel Davenport.

Episode 7 of the season, *The Birdman of Wormwood Scrubs,* was the first to be written by Leon Griffiths since his stroke. In a matter of two years he had fought back from being barely able to communicate or fend for himself to being able to write again for television. His mark can be clearly seen. Stand-up comedian Max Wall appears in the episode in a rare straight role as a prisoner who is released after a long prison term and sets out to recover the nest egg he deposited in a bank before his arrest. Actress Rula Lenska made the first of three appearances in *Minder* in this episode as a corrupt model.

Rula Lenska

Rula Lenska was the daughter of a Polish count and countess. Tall, glamorous and with stunning red hair, she had had some acting success in the 1976 Thames Television series *Rock Follies*, about a trio of female pop singers. She had also become something of a cult figure across the Atlantic in the late seventies when she appeared in a television commercial for Alberto VO5 Hot Oil Treatment and proclaimed to puzzled millions, 'I'm Rula Lenska,' in a manner suggesting that the name should mean something to them. There were even Rula Lenska look-alike competitions on American television and jokes about her on the Johnny Carson show.[8]

Following her appearance on *Minder* she became romantically involved with Dennis Waterman and there was a highly publicised break-up of their existing marriages. The tabloid press lapped it up, with endless headlines referring to 'The Cockney and the Countess'.

Waterman had already been through one divorce (from first wife Penny), and the publicity surrounding his separation from his current wife Patricia Maynard and their two daughters created a highly emotional and traumatic episode in his life. He had reached a high spot in his career through *The Sweeney* and now *Minder*, and was a highly visible public personality. The tabloid scandal was particularly hard to handle, but both he and Lenska did so with dignity and fortitude. The couple were married in Western Australia in January 1987, but sadly that marriage also ended in divorce a few years later.

Minder *enters the language*

Episode 11 of the third season was *Poetic Justice, Innit* by Tony Hoare, a particular classic in the style of Sidney Lumet's *Twelve Angry Men*. Arthur is elected jury foreman in a case of handling stolen property and finds himself too easily able to identify with the defendant.

Two weeks later Arthur himself was in the frame in Leon Griffiths' *In*, in which he was suspected of having imported a second-hand car containing illicit drugs from the continent.

The third season marked a turning point for the show and it began to make regular appearances in the 'top ten' television charts, twice reaching as high as number four. Asked later to nominate the high point in the show's run, George Cole replied: 'The third series when we got into the ratings for the first time.'

By now, a number of Arthur's catch-phrases had found their way into common use: 'a nice little earner', 'stand on me, Terry', and 'a word in your shell-like' being some of the more popular.

Arthur had also established himself as a master of malapropism. Among his gems were 'I was a mere prawn in the game', and 'using a prat to catch a mackerel'. He would refer to a priest as 'your honour' and, like a naughty schoolboy, would reply 'yes miss' after a dressing down from a female magistrate. In one episode he asked of another character: 'How would you have fared in the Blitz with bombs raining down from the Lufthansa?'

George Cole described how one of the most popular catch-phrases came about. He recalls: 'My son, who is a scriptwriter, came round one afternoon and said, "I've just heard someone in a pub come out with a great Arthur Daley line." I gave him £25 and said, "Don't use it. Keep that one for me." I kept it for a couple of years until the right time came along and we eventually used it in the episode about boxing. Leon Griffiths, who wrote the episode, came up to me afterwards and said, "I think I owe you £12.50".' The line was first heard in Episode 39, *Rocky Eight and a Half* when Arthur Daley congratulates Terry on winning a boxing bout and tells him, 'The world is your lobster, my son.'

Cockney rhyming slang and London street slang were used liberally in the programme's dialogue. Examples that were well established in London, such as porkies (pork pies = lies) and boracic (boracic lint = skint, i.e. poor), were introduced to the wider audience, together with some of the more obscure examples. How many viewers were left wondering long after the episode finished how a watch could become a kettle? (Kettle on the hob = fob, hence an abbreviation for fob watch.) Or how backside becomes Aris? (Aris is an abbreviation for Aristotle, which is rhyming slang for bottle, which itself is an abbreviation for 'bottle and glass' = arse.) Or iron for a homosexual? (Iron hoof = poof.)

Much of the rhyming slang was genuine, albeit obscure. But much was contrived. Arthur was well known for his appreciation of a vodka and tonic ('Gimme a large V.A.T., Dave' — coincidentally having the initials of the despised British value added tax). Often he would use the somewhat contrived rhyming slang 'Vera and Philharmonic' for gin and tonic — Vera as rhyming slang for gin, after British wartime singer Vera Lynn.

Andrew Payne's *Get Daley!* in Season 4 contained a marvellous example of made-up slang when a patient in the next bed to Arthur in hospital said he was there to have his 'Chalfonts' done. From Chalfont St Giles (a place north of London): hence piles i.e. haemorrhoids. (More *Minder* slang is explained in the glossary on page 75.)

Cockney comedian Arthur Mullard complained: 'There's no such thing as rhyming slang these days. It's all down to modern scriptwriters.'[9] He could easily have added 'and the pressure to come up with something new each week for long-running shows like *EastEnders* and *The Bill*.'

When final production of Season 3 had been completed, the cast and crew had their traditional wrap-up party and no one knew if they would be together again for a new season. George Cole remarked: 'There were contracts with the company for each individual series. We would be commissioned to do one series and that was that. Then after the series was finished they would come back and ask us if we were interested in doing another one.'

The season was a great success. But it was 20 months before the programme was back on the air.

Meanwhile, a second novelty record tying in to the programme and using typical expressions from *Minder's* dialogue was *Arthur Daley ('e's Alright)* by the Firm, which reached number 14 in the charts in August 1982.

Season 4   26 December 1983–21 March 1984

Despite whispers that Cole and Waterman were considering leaving the series, the show reappeared on Boxing Day 1983 with a special Christmas edition containing clips from some of the earlier episodes linked by a loose story line. This episode was in fact the prelude to the fourth season that began in January 1984. Joint producer of the previous three seasons Lloyd Shirley had now joined Verity Lambert as co-executive producer. George Taylor remained as producer. Some of the previous season's sparkle still remained and there were some very amusing episodes, such as *Senior Citizen Caine* by Andrew Payne, in which television veteran Lionel Jeffries arrives for his character's wife's funeral on a motorbike wearing goggles and gloves, and has a Walkman plugged in his ears during the service.

Sorry Pal, Wrong Number, by Leon Griffiths, was another classic from the fourth season in which Arthur teams up with a con man (played by T P McKenna) to start a racing tips business and commandeers three public telephone boxes on a railway station from which to operate. This episode also found its way into another of *Minder's* written tie-ins. The book, entitled simply *Minder*, by Anthony Masters and published by Sphere Books in 1984, declared itself to be a novel but consisted essentially of the dialogue from three of Leon Griffiths' episodes (*You Gotta Have Friends; Rocky Eight and a Half; and Sorry Pal, Wrong Number*) plus a short story that was never made into an episode. Two more *Minder* 'novels' by Anthony Masters were released during the 1980s: *Minder — Back Again*, and *Minder — Yet Again!*

Although the show was now approaching the peak of its popularity, twice reaching number two in the charts during the fourth season, the plots were beginning to outgrow the format for which they were being created. Some of the episodes were quite mediocre and tedious while others, such as *Windows*, by Geoff Case, still managed to achieve a comfortable balance of fun and drama for the 52 minutes available. Such was the show's success, however, that the fourth season that ended in March 1984 was followed just six months later by a fifth season of nine episodes.

Season 5   *5 September–26 December 1984*

In April 1984, during the break between the fourth and fifth seasons of *Minder*, Thames Television International received an award for 'TV franchise' under the *Queen's Awards for Export Achievement* in recognition of its generating an export income of £18 million the previous year from sales of *Minder, The Benny Hill Show, Rumpole of the Bailey* and more.[10]

The fifth season started on 5 September 1984 with great fanfare but a slightly disappointing episode entitled *Goodbye Sailor*, by Andrew Payne, involving contraband tobacco smuggled by boat from the continent. One of the highlights came at the end of the episode when Chisholm came into the Winchester Club and found a suspicious-looking holdall on the floor next to Arthur. He was supposed to unzip it and discover that it contained a life raft that inflates in front of him. Patrick Malahide takes up the story:

> Before the take, I check it out with the first assistant director, and as usual, he tells me we've only time for one take and no rehearsal. But he calls over the man who supplies the life raft, and he tells me there's nothing to worry about — it just flops open and inflates slowly. So they turn over the camera and I stalk into the bar, beady eyes clock the bag, I step astride it, unzip it, and bang! The bloody thing explodes! Nearly

blew my legs apart! And I keep going until they say 'cut'. The producer gave me a gin and tonic that night, the first and only time. I think they thought I would sue them.

Three episodes in the season reached the coveted number one position in the television charts, a tribute particularly to Lloyd Shirley who was now the sole executive producer and George Taylor who was the producer.

Some of the episodes in the fifth season were excellent. The second episode, *What Makes Shamy Run?* by Leon Griffiths, was one of them. This episode featured ex-dancer Fred Evans whose refreshingly over-the-top character uses counterfeit banknotes to buy an up-to-date Roger Moore-style wig to replace his outdated Engelbert Humperdinck one. The episode also enlightened the viewing public that syrup (short for 'syrup of fig'), and Irish (for 'Irish jig'), were cockney rhyming slang for wig.

This was a classic Leon Griffiths episode. The main story line concerned a stolen master copy of an Indian movie, but what so often happened in Griffiths' stories was that the subplots overtook the main story line. In this episode we find ourselves laughing about wigs and counterfeit bank notes while the main story line becomes of secondary importance.

The following week saw Tony Hoare's amusing episode *A Number of Old Wives' Tales* featuring Patrick Mower (Detective Superintendent Steve Hackett of BBC-1's *Target*), whose character invites Terry to be best man at his wedding — without revealing that he has four other wives scattered around the country.

The Second Time Around, by Geoffrey Case, concerning second-hand furniture and romantic relationships gone sour, was a rather hard-going episode that not even guest artists Beryl Reid and Bill Maynard were fully able to save.

Tony Hoare's *Second Hand Pose*, the following week, again showed that a complicated story line did not automatically mean a better episode. In this episode, Terry decides to find other employment after being locked in a freezer when one of Arthur's schemes goes wrong. Leon Griffiths' episode *The Long Ride Back to Scratchwood* brought things back on track with a story about football ticket scalping.

In the final three episodes of the season, we see Arthur involved with a hypnotist, a greyhound that refuses to run, and an attempt to become elected to the local council.

Overall, the episodes in the fifth season were adequate but some just seemed to lack that special sparkle and gave the impression that the producers were trying too hard. To make matters worse, programming schedules for the last few episodes were disrupted by an industrial dispute, which meant that some regions missed out on some episodes and other episodes went out at odd times.

The season closed with a Boxing Day Special in 1984 (Tony Hoare's *Around the Corner* about the temperamental greyhound) and there was a nine-month break before the start of the sixth season.

Season 6   4 September–25 December 1985

In February 1985, two months after the end of the fifth season, George Cole and Dennis Waterman received awards from the Variety Club of Great Britain as joint ITV personalities of the year for their performances in *Minder*. Creator Leon Griffiths also received an award from the British Association of Film and Television Arts (BAFTA) for his writing on the series.

A few months later, the newly-introduced personal computer technology caught up with the programme and a *Minder* computer game was released by DK'Tronics in June 1985. Written by Don Priestley, the game was authorised by Thames Television and carried its logo on the package along with a photo of Cole and Waterman. The object of the game was for the player, in the role of Arthur, to collect stock with the help of Terry and Dave and to avoid Chisholm when the goods were hookey. By today's standards, the game's graphics appear crude and clumsy, but given what was available at the time, it provided an entertaining and imaginative family game. Through the benefit of the worldwide web, an on-line version of the game can still be played (*www.minder.org*).

The industry awards and the nine-month break between seasons had obviously made a difference. The series bounced back in September 1985 for what was, strictly speaking, a half-season of six episodes. First off was a hilarious episode by Andrew Payne entitled *Give Us This Day Arthur Daley's Bread*. This involved a group of ex-prisoners who Arthur employs as landscape gardeners but who use the opportunity to engage in some petty burglary. This classic episode featured the highly amusing James Booth as leader of the group — with his affectation to include the term 'blah, blah, blah, b'boom' in his speech — and Norman Eshley as the naïve but well-meaning vicar who takes the ex-prisoners under his wing.

Life in the Fast Food Lane, by Alistair Beaton, the following week contained some almost slapstick comedy as Arthur and Terry attempt to remove coloured stickers from the phones in a telephone shop to put onto the dodgy car-phones that Arthur is trying to shift. Alongside the comedy was a return to the violence of previous days when Terry gets on the wrong side of a vicious fight.

Two weeks later, *Arthur is Dead, Long Live Arthur,* by Tony Hoare, saw Arthur hiding out in a boarding house run by a lonely widow (played by George Cole's real-life wife Penny Morrell), after faking his suicide because he is unable to face paying a £20,000 tax bill. There are some very amusing sequences during the episode as Arthur checks out various possibilities for his mode of suicide and plans his funeral with an undertaker.

In *From Fulham with Love,* also by Tony Hoare, Arthur is selling dodgy gear to the crew of a Russian ship and gets involved in a possible defection by one of the crew members. This was the second episode in which Rula Lenska appeared, this time as the ship's bosun. Also memorable from this episode is a hilarious performance by Jonathan Warren as Arthur's skinhead nephew Nigel with a swastika tattooed on his forehead. Not everyone agreed that Nigel's appearance was strictly necessary. Mark Lawson, in *The Times,* considered it 'the product of desperation, not necessity'.[11]

The final episode in the season, *Waiting for Goddard* by Leon Griffiths, featured an ageing Ronald Fraser as an eccentric recluse who comes into some money that Arthur wants to take an unreasonable cut from. The episode ended with a cliffhanger in which Terry again walks out on Arthur after an argument. This would have been a good place for the series to end. All the indications were that the show was indeed over, following more rumours that Cole and Waterman were pulling out.

Writing in *The Times* about *Waiting for Goddard,* Mark Lawson said that apart from a two-hour Christmas special, the episode 'will almost certainly be the last'.[11] Describing Leon Griffiths' original concept of *Minder,* Lawson quoted Griffiths as saying that he initially wanted 'a cynicism which would reflect the times in which we live,' but six years later he had obtained 'a kind of Boulting Brothers thing' that had gone back to the kind of comedy they set out to avoid.

Apparently disillusioned about the direction the programme had taken, this was the final episode of the show written by Griffiths. The programme was at the peak of its success. But Lawson summed up the views of many when he wrote: 'It is better that *Minder* goes now. Once you could smell the sweat, but now it comes round doused with the deodorant of popular acclaim.'"

Linda Agran, script executive at Euston Films, describes in Dennis Waterman's autobiography how the series started out as a tough drama with some comedy but, bit by bit, the comedy took over: 'Leon and I were both concerned,' she said. 'Three series had been enough. The writers had used up the best ideas, the most exciting story lines, but Thames wouldn't have it.' She went on: 'What a shame *Minder* was not killed off at its peak. Instead it was allowed to die slowly in front of the public.'"

Two months after *Waiting for Goddard* the show was back with a two-hour feature film, *Minder on the Orient Express,* shown on Christmas Day 1985. Written by Andrew Payne, this featured all the regulars, including Chisholm and Rycott and their respective sidekicks, Detective Constables Jones and Melish, together with Glynn Edwards as Dave and co-stars Honor Blackman, Adam Faith and Robert Beatty. With this cast it could easily have been a farewell. It looked as if it was. Thames Television even authorised the publication of *Minder Annual 1986* by World International Publishing Limited. This was a 63-page stocking-filler for the 1985 Christmas season consisting of some stock photographs of Cole and Waterman, several line drawings and some short stories involving the *Minder* characters without any writer credits.

In 1986, George Cole won the *TV Times* best actor award for his portrayal of Arthur, although by now both he and Waterman had become involved in other projects. Cole had already appeared in the 1985 BBC-2 series *Blott on the Landscape* based on Tom Sharpe's book of the same name.

The following year Waterman appeared as Bobbo, a philandering husband, in the bizarre BBC-2 four-part miniseries *The Life and Loves of a She Devil.* Adapted from Fay Weldon's novel, the programme saw him cast alongside Julie T. Wallace, who played his ex-wife, the she-devil of the title, who inflicts a series of punishments upon him, and Patricia Hodge as his new love interest. But apart from occasional repeats, *Minder* was off the air for three years. Christmas of 1986 was the first for five years without a *Minder* being shown over the holiday season. Waterman in the meantime had gone to

Australia with his new partner Rula Lenska where they performed together in Tom Stoppard's play *The Real Thing.*

Adding to the general feeling of closure, *TV Times* had run a competition to award Arthur Daley's Jaguar as a prize in a competition. (Parenthetically, the car became a celebrity in its own right. The competition winner subsequently had it auctioned for charity in aid of Hospice Care, Salisbury and raised £10,000. At the time of writing, the car is being auctioned once again in support of Hospice Care, this time on the Internet.)

Season 7   26 December 1988–6 February 1989

The viewing public had largely accepted that *Minder's* days were over. It came as a pleasant surprise, therefore, when a new *Minder* feature film was shown on Boxing Day 1988, three years after the most recent episode. *An Officer and a Car Salesman,* by Tony Hoare, was a 90-minute feature film as a prelude to the seventh season (also a half season of six episodes) that began in the new year. In *An Officer and a Car Salesman* Terry had just been released after an 18-month prison term resulting from Arthur having stored stolen video players at Terry's flat without his knowledge. The relationship between Terry and Arthur was now noticeably strained.

One of the most significant changes in the new season was that Euston Films had decided to drop the Chisholm character without explanation. A furore in the press ensued when word got out that Chisholm was no longer to appear. There was even a phone-in campaign organised by a national radio station, with the Euston Films switchboard being swamped with calls. They were eventually forced to concede that the character would return in the Christmas Special. Which he did. And named his own fee.

In retrospect, it still seems an odd decision to axe a member of the team who was so hugely popular with the audience. Perhaps it was felt that the relationship between Arthur Daley and Chisholm was in some way upsetting the balance of the show.

Whatever the reason, Chisholm's character appeared for the last time in *An Officer and a Car Salesman* as chief security officer in a private security firm, Chisholm having been forced to retire from the police force after an enquiry into his overzealous interest in Arthur's activities.

Patrick Malahide said later: 'I was angry at the time, but kept it to myself, and decided to leave with dignity. It turned out to be a blessing in disguise, as I was never trapped in the series and was able to move on to other things.'

The 'other things' to which he referred would certainly include the BBC-2 mini-series *Middlemarch*, adapted from George Eliot's 1871 novel, BBC-1's *The Inspector Alleyn Mysteries*, in which he played the title role as a 1940s police officer, as well as a number of successful film roles such as *December Bride* (1993), *A Man of No Importance* (1994) and *The Long Kiss Goodnight* (1996).

Peter Childs remained in the new season in his role as Rycott, as did Michael Povey as Chisholm's ex-sidekick Jones, now promoted to Detective Sergeant. The season returned with its successful format of bringing in familiar guest artists for each episode. *It's a Sorry Lorry, Morrie*, by Tony Hoare, saw reappearances by Ronald Fraser and Roy Kinnear (sadly, just before his death). The story involved Terry driving a lorry-load of electrical goods for Arthur, unaware that they were stolen.

Days of Fines and Closures, by David Yallop, which went out the following week, had the makings of a true thriller when Dave from the Winchester Club mysteriously failed to return from a day trip to Folkestone

This episode was produced at the height of the affair between Dennis Waterman and Rula Lenska. Waterman's wife at the time, Pat Maynard, appears in the episode as Dave's wife. She has an amusing scene in which she arrives at court blaming Arthur for Dave's disappearance and hits him with her handbag. She describes in Dennis Waterman's autobiography what a strange experience it was when none of the crew laughed. She couldn't understand why the crew was behaving so strangely to her.[12]

Fatal Impression, by Anita Bronson, was the only episode in the entire run of the series that was wholly credited to a female writer. This episode co-starred Billy Connolly as an on-course bookmaker who, along with Arthur and several others, is owed money by a reformed gambler who has just died. This episode also featured television veteran Sheila Steafel as a pub singer.

Andrew Payne's *The Last Video Show* featured Ian McShane as a high-flying criminal and Brian Blessed as a corrupt police officer who are caught together on an amateur video in a compromising situation. Also featured was Rula Lenska in her third appearance in the series, this time as the criminal's wife. *Fiddler on the Hoof*, by David Humphries, brought in Don Henderson, still highly recognisable after his *Bulmer* role, and Gerald Campion (famed for his *Billy Bunter* role in the 1950s) in a minor part as a café proprietor.

The last episode in the season, *The Wrong Goodbye* by David Yallop, saw an appearance of Paul Eddington as a corrupt property developer, together with all the regulars including Mark Farmer in his role as Justin and Royce Mills as Arthur's slightly camp accountant Andrew. Sadly, this was the last appearance of Peter Childs as Detective Sergeant Rycott. He died of leukaemia later in the year at the age of 50.[13]

The season had its high spots (such as Rycott accidentally setting fire to a lorry doused in petrol in *It's a Sorry Lorry, Morrie*) but generally the plots were cumbersome and the magic ingredient from the early seasons was sadly lacking. A distinct chasm had opened between Arthur and Terry. After his latest spell in prison, Terry had become more aware of Arthur's manipulation of him and was now more prepared than at any other time to say no. In Anita Bronson's *Fatal Impression*, Terry actually finds himself a job in a car showroom, despite Arthur's attempts to foil his chances before the interview. Once again the audience finds itself feeling total contempt for Arthur and sympathy for Terry — yet bewilderment as to why he continues to take it. We never find out whether Terry actually started work in the showroom.

Lynne Truss, writing in *The Times*, considered this period the nadir of the series: 'The souring relationship between the treacherous Arthur and the exploited Terry was like watching someone whip a dog. I never trusted Arthur after that.'[14]

By the end of the seventh season Dennis Waterman decided that enough was enough. Over the years, the language on the show had been gradually toned down to accommodate new standards of political correctness and had diluted much of the crisp dialogue of earlier episodes. On top of this there was a serious debate raging about whether the depiction of violence on television was contributing to the rising level of violence in society. Waterman describes in his autobiography how this stopped him from 'actually being a minder' and says, 'with absolutely no hint of jealousy,' that the show had become 'The Arthur Daley Comedy Hour'.[12] He had a discussion with producer George Taylor, who also had concerns about the scripts, and decided to quit at the end of the seventh season to take on some new projects. These included Yorkshire Television's *Stay Lucky* series of comedy thrillers beginning in 1989 and an unconvincing lead role in the 1990 BBC-1 sit-com

On the Up as cockney self-made millionaire Tony Carpenter. But it seemed that *Minder* had come to an end. Even the title of the last episode, *The Wrong Goodbye*, suggested that it was all over. The programme was off the screen for two and a half years.

Season 8 — A new Minder   *5 September–25 December 1991*

To their credit, Euston Films took the courageous step of bringing the programme back for an eighth series two-and-a-half years later with a new minder. To die-hard fans this was heresy. The minder *was* Dennis Waterman, and the notion of having someone else in the role was unthinkable. Audience and trade predictions were that the idea was doomed to failure. But the producers stood their ground and cast 26-year-old Gary Webster in the role of Ray, Arthur's nephew, who Arthur takes on as his new minder.

Adding to the risk was the fact that Webster was already well known to viewers from his role as Graham in ten episodes of *EastEnders*. There was a distinct possibility of a repeat of the confusion that beset viewers in the first season when Dennis Waterman was still strongly identified with his previous role in *The Sweeney*. To soften the blow another literary tie-in was authorised, this time the supposed autobiography of Arthur Daley. *Straight Up* by Arthur Daley 'as told to Paul Ableman' was published by Mandarin in 1991.

George Cole said later: 'When I heard that Dennis didn't want to do another series I said I wouldn't work without him. Forty-eight hours later Euston Films came back and said they didn't agree. They felt it would work with a new minder. If they were prepared to take the chance so was I. I think David Yallop's script helped it to work. By having Gary Webster play one of the family Arthur was more lumbered than ever. Gary Webster was excellent.'

But Dennis Waterman echoed the sentiments of many people: 'I thought they were a bit stupid to retain the title. It was daft to keep calling it *Minder* after the minder had gone.'[15]

Stupid or not, the first episode in the new format went out on 5 September 1991, the first in a season of 13 episodes. To the amazement of most, the formula was successful and ran for three seasons in the new format.

In the first episode, *The Loneliness of the Long Distance Entrepreneur*, by David A. Yallop, Arthur discovers that Terry has got married and gone to Australia. In urgent need of a general assistant, Arthur reluctantly takes on his nephew

Ray, the son of Arthur's brother Bert. But when word gets out that Arthur is without a minder, he and Dave receive a visit at the Winchester Club from some heavies wanting to offer some protection. Ray diffuses the situation and shows that he is able to handle himself and Arthur elevates him to minder. The remainder of the story involves a drug smuggling operation using cars imported by Arthur.

Writer David A. Yallop said at the time: 'The new character had to be more than Terry, Mark II. Ray is a man of the Nineties, more intelligent and cynical, and that opens up a new seam of humour. I think we pulled off one of the most difficult tricks, re-assembling a partnership, injecting new life in the process. If George Cole decided to stop, however, we might have to call it a day.'[16]

With the new season, the programme underwent a major revamp. The opening credits were played over film of Arthur and Ray walking through Soho. The closing title sequence showed them walking along the mile-long pier at Southend-on-Sea, famed as the longest seaside pier in the world. When they reach the end of the pier, Arthur realises he has left something behind and they have to turn around and walk back again. The theme music was a new version of *I Could Be So Good For You* without vocals, and George Cole had first billing in the credits.

John Hambley, who had been executive producer since the second feature film in 1988 continued in that role for the new season and the two that followed. All 36 new episodes were produced by Ian Toynton, who had been credited as director on eight of the earlier ones and associate producer of many. Several new directors were employed on the new episodes including Diarmuid Lawrence, Roger Bamford, Gordon Flemyng and Lawrence Gordon Clark who, between them, directed 23 episodes.

The new season also saw the recruitment of several new writers. Bernard Dempsey and Kevin Sperring co-wrote nine, William Ivory wrote eight, Iain Roy and Chris Kelly co-wrote two, and Tony Jordan wrote two (one with Liane Clark). There were also a number of single episodes from new writers. The writers from the previous seasons were not left out, and David A. Yallop, who had written three episodes in earlier seasons, wrote seven of the new ones. Veteran television writer Tony Hoare, with 17 episodes to his credit from previous seasons, wrote another three, including the final episode and the one-hundredth.

Nicholas Day (DS Morley)

The scripts were generally excellent and the stories were able to sustain themselves without the need to bring in familiar guest artists. Arthur Daley had obviously had some success and was running a respectable car business 'Daley into Europe Ltd' which imported used cars from the continent. He was not simply a member of the Winchester Club but now a 25 percent shareholder. Business at the lockup still occupied much of his time, but the lockup was now in Willesden rather than Fulham. (No reason was given for its new location.) In this and the next season, his nemesis in the local police was Detective Sergeant Morley (played by Nicholas Day), assisted by Detective Constable Park (Stephen Tompkinson) in Season 8 and Detective Constable Field (Jonty Stephens) in Season 9. (Park and Field? Where was the writers' imagination?) There was no regular police presence in Season 10, the last season, although we did see the appearance of a less formal style of detective (described by Arthur as 'plod with ponytails') in two episodes.

Nicholas Day who played Detective Sergeant Morley was a late replacement. He had been booked to play a small part as a greyhound trainer in one episode but the producers decided on a last-minute change of roles and asked him to audition as a police officer. He told the *TV Times:* 'By the time I went to bed I was playing DS Morley, had a six-month contract and a car would be picking me up on Monday to start work!' To prepare for the role at short notice, he went to his local police station in South London and asked to meet a detective. He said that as soon as he mentioned *Minder,* 'doors just seemed to open.'[17]

He remembers: 'They had already shot two episodes so I had to re-shoot any policeman scenes in those episodes while George and Dennis were shooting Episode 3 scenes that I wasn't in. So when you see me in those two episodes talking to either George or Dennis they were not actually there! I watched recordings so I knew roughly what they did and then talked to thin air.'

Day said later: 'The great challenge for me was to be funny *and* believable. They had great difficulty casting this role and I knew that there would be another candidate for the role queuing up behind me.

'I remember the pressure of that first day. I was replacing another actor and was thrown into the middle of shooting. I had to walk downstairs into the Winchester and act with people I had barely been introduced to. I remember coming down the stairs on "Action" and saying the wrong line to the wrong person at the wrong time.

'They let me do my own stunt driving in a car chase for the first series, which was great fun. On the second series they decided the insurance wouldn't allow it — so a stunt driver dressed up as me would screech to a halt and I would leap out from behind the car!'

The language of the new stories also underwent a subtle change. There was no particular emphasis on London argot. Slang was used where appropriate, but it was no longer constantly reinforcing the idea that the characters were Londoners. Whole episodes would go by without rhyming slang being uttered.

Additionally, the new episodes did not dwell on the role of Ray as a minder. Ray was family: someone to run the business when Arthur was not around. He was the heir apparent to Arthur's business — which seemed a little odd, given that Arthur had two children of his own. And Ray was totally loyal to Arthur. The worst thing that anyone could do while Ray was around was to slight the Daley family name. He had had a difficult childhood, with his father in prison, but Arthur had always looked after him. Now he was paying Arthur back.

Many of the story lines revolved around the Daley family. Arthur's stuttering brother Bert (Ray's father) played by Sidney Livingstone, and Bert's domineering wife Doreen (Lill Roughley) featured prominently. Sidney Livingstone, who played Bert in eight episodes, was not actually a newcomer to the series having already appeared as a different character ten years earlier.

The writers came up with a variety of new ideas for the 13 episodes of the new season, together with a rehash of some old ones. The first episode in the new format, *The Loneliness of the Long Distance Entrepreneur*, begins with a wedding in the Daley family. 'Er indoors was cleverly not shown. She had retired to a bedroom to overcome the humiliation of being seen in an exclusive dress obtained by Arthur that several of the other guests were also wearing. Two weeks later, in David A. Yallop's *Whatever Happened to Her Indoors*, she went missing and the local police suspect Arthur of having committed a serious crime. Kevin McNally, credited with a small part in this episode, is actually Kevin Sperring who wrote several episodes with Bernard Dempsey.

A Bouquet of Barbed Wine, by Kevin Sperring and Bernard Dempsey, saw Arthur dabbling in wine once again after his previous attempts in the second season. This time we find him suspended in a lift well overnight when he tries to return a batch of stolen wine to a warehouse when he discovers that the wine is corked. In David A. Yallop's *Three Cons Make a Mountain*, he finds himself the victim of three con tricks perpetrated by a trio of villains he has cheated over the years. This episode also sees him performing a credible rendition of *My Way*.

Guess Who's Coming to Pinner, by David A. Yallop, was a slightly surreal episode in which Arthur was invited by a big-time villain to take part in a major job but was too drunk to remember any details. *The Last Temptation of Daley* the following week saw Arthur unable to cope with life when his doctor orders him to give up alcohol and tobacco. This episode saw a rehash of an idea used in an early episode in which a disgruntled customer is after Arthur for a refund on some tins of paint that Arthur sold him.

One of the more novel ideas was in *The Greatest Show in Willesden*, by Kevin Sperring and Bernard Dempsey, in which John Cater (doorman Starr from

The Duchess of Duke Street) appeared as an ageing ventriloquist whom Arthur brings in to generate additional business at an ailing pub. *The Coach That Came in from the Cold*, by Kevin Clark, was an amusing, if rather implausible story, about Arthur buying a ex-police coach from the local police division, hoping to get into the coach tour business.

The season ended with a special on Christmas Day 1991, *The Cruel Canal*, by Kevin Sperring and Bernard Dempsey, in which Arthur and Ray find themselves transporting a load of video players on a barge through London's canal system. Memorable from this episode is a game of Monopoly played by Arthur and Ray on the barge and the sight of Dave from the Winchester Club travelling at high speed along the Grand Union Canal in a motorboat trying to locate them. Glynn Edwards recalls: 'We got in a lot of trouble over that. You're not supposed to make a wash and there is a five-mile-an-hour speed limit. But I think we managed to smooth it out with the authorities by the end of the afternoon and there was no harm done.'

Minder had triumphed again. After a three-year break the programme was back in prime time over the Christmas holiday season. But this was a different *Minder*. These were stories about Arthur Daley. The minder, Ray, was largely peripheral to the stories. But the viewers loved it. Another 13 episodes went into production in 1992 in preparation for the ninth season beginning on 7 January 1993.

Season 9   *7 January–1 April 1993*

Leon Griffiths died in June 1992 following additional strokes and a brain tumour. He was 64. By that time, Season 9 was already well into production. What bounced back onto our television screens on 7 January 1993 was very different from Leon Griffiths' original concept.

The season opened with *I'll Never Forget Whats 'Ername*, the second episode of eight written by William Ivory (the first was *The Last Temptation of Daley* in Season 8). This was a 'feel good' episode in which Arthur, Ray and Dave take part as a team in a quiz night at the Winchester Club with Arthur trying to recruit an escapee from an open prison as the other team member.

Violence, or at least implied violence, reappeared the following week in Tim Firth's *No Way to Treat a Daley*. Arthur innocently attempts to set up an advertising business using an aerial balloon and finds himself in serious danger from a businessman known for his sadistic treatment of competitors. The close family bond between Arthur and Ray is never more clearly seen than in this episode. The way in which Ray deals with the businessman and reduces him to a sobbing wreck is a little over the top but leaves no doubt as to the lengths he is prepared to go to protect his uncle.

This is in fact a very sensitive episode that teaches us a lot about Arthur. While he is being held captive overnight Arthur senses that Warren, his captor, is far from happy working for his merciless boss. Arthur skilfully uses his own life experiences to bring out Warren's problems and to demonstrate to Warren that he does not have to spend his life the way he does. Arthur's dialogue with Warren is expertly crafted to maintain an element of his dry humour while slowly building up Warren's confidence so that they can both get out of the situations in which they have found themselves. This episode is *Minder* at its best and fully demonstrates the artistry that George Cole had developed from half a century of acting.

Over the next three episodes we see humour when Arthur sets up a courier business in *Uneasy Rider*, by Geoff Rowley. A scene in which Arthur feigns interest in the preachings of two Jehovah's Witnesses to buy time for someone to rescue him from a thug is hilarious. There is more humour in *Looking for Mr. Goodtime* when he defends himself in court on a charge of propositioning a woman in the street. In *Opportunity Knocks and Bruises* he is outsmarted on a deal with a fairground owner but outsmarts him in return, and enjoys himself at the fair along the way. We also see Arthur make a lame attempt at political correctness when he addresses the chairwoman of the Neighbourhood Watch Committee as 'madam chair-human'.

In Bernard Dempsey and Kevin Sperring's *Gone with the Winchester*, the close friendship between Arthur and Dave is almost torn apart when another member of their boyhood gang appears at the Winchester after a long prison sentence and causes Arthur to start questioning Dave's loyalty. Also in this episode we see Arthur speaking with genuine affection for 'er indoors as he reminisces with Dave about their courting days. We learn that she and Arthur were married in 1953, Queen Elizabeth's coronation year, went to Shoebury-ness for their honeymoon and that Arthur acquired a pitch for a snack stall in Trafalgar Square on Coronation Day.

The season ended with a trilogy of episodes involving a potential bequest to Arthur following the death of a possible relative in Australia. The first episode of the three was set in England and dealt with Arthur's attempts to prove his relationship to a deceased person he had never heard of. The second and third parts were made on location in Sydney in collaboration with the Australian Broadcasting Corporation. These dealt with Arthur and Ray's attempts to claim the inheritance and their troubles along the way. Fussy viewers were no doubt able to see through the holes, ('How could someone get on a plane from England to Australia without a return ticket?') but the location idea was a great success, especially with Australian viewers.

Season 10 — *The end of the road*   6 January–10 March 1994

Following Leon Griffiths' death in June 1992, the decision was taken to bring the show to an end. In October 1993 Euston Films announced that *Minder* would cease production at the end of the tenth season. John Hambley, the show's executive producer said: 'When you get past the 100th episode, it becomes increasingly difficult to think of original stories and ideas.'[18] That may have been so, but that is why we have scriptwriters. In reality, Thames Television had lost its franchise, and hence its broadcasting licence, to Carlton Communications and there was no guarantee that, even if it were made, another franchise holder would buy the series.

The final season opened on 6 January 1994 with *A Fridge Too Far*, by Bernard Dempsey and Kevin Sperring, in which Arthur stages a robbery at the lockup to claim on an insurance policy. In William Ivory's *Another Case of Van Blank*, we see Arthur, Ray and Dave travel to France to take advantage of relaxed restrictions on the importation of liquor, and Arthur's ensuing arrest for unwittingly being present when his liquor order is stolen from a warehouse. We also see that even Arthur is not averse to a little flirting when he meets a French woman (played by Mylene Demongeot) who mistakes him for an old flame.

The 100th episode, *All Things Brighton Beautiful*, went to air on 20 January 1994. To be strictly accurate, this was the 101st episode. The 1983 Christmas special made up of clips from previous episodes was not counted as a full episode in the final tally. To celebrate the occasion, Tony Hoare, the longest-serving writer on the series, was invited to provide the story. He came up with an implausible theme in which an old acquaintance of Arthur's has himself delivered to the lockup in a packing case seeking refuge for a couple of weeks from what he claims is a menacing skinhead who is out to kill him. Arthur arranges for him to stay in a caravan in Brighton, but the caravan explodes and they find themselves in a Salvation Army hostel.

The opening and closing credit sequences were changed specially. The opening credits were played over film of the packing case being delivered to the lockup. The closing sequence saw a bedraggled Arthur in the congregation of the hostel singing *Onward Christian Soldiers* along with a brass band accompaniment. Despite the special treatment, the episode was rather weak but benefited greatly from the casting of the talented Andrew Sachs (Manuel from *Fawlty Towers*) as the man in the packing case.

The following week's episode, *One Flew Over the Parent's Nest*, by Tony Hoare, was indistinguishable in style from his episodes ten years earlier. Terry McCann could easily have been substituted for Ray Daley and no one would have known the difference. Without their knowledge, Arthur lets out Bert and Doreen's house to a young girl to whom Ray had given a lift from the airport. As a result Arthur finds himself arrested for running a brothel when it transpires that the girl is a high-class call girl.

Next in the season we saw Arthur taking confession after he sold a car to a nun at a greatly inflated price (*The Immaculate Contraption* by William Ivory). In *All Quiet on the West End Front*, by Bernard Dempsey and Kevin Sperring, Arthur opens an executive entertainment business. His banter with a ticket tout for *Les Misérables* is priceless.

In *The Great Depression of 1994*, by Arthur Ellis, Arthur's brother-in-law, feigns an attack of depression to try to stop Ray's mother interfering in their life. We see Arthur dabbling as a psychological counsellor. The whole theme of the story was depression, and the audience was left wondering what was the point of it all.

The following week saw the return of humour in *On the Autofront*, by William Ivory. Here we see Arthur employ the services of two black rappers to make a radio commercial when there is a slump in his used-car sales. In the same episode he is threatened with a charge of attempted murder after being driven through the window of an antique shop by a competing car dealer who takes one of Arthur's cars on a test drive. There is more trouble with the police in *Bring Me the Head of Arthur Daley*, by Bernard Dempsey and Kevin Sperring. In this episode Arthur is sentenced to community service after a stolen carpet is planted in the lockup as revenge by a long-term prisoner who believes that Arthur is responsible for his capture. Stratford Johns of *Softly, Softly* and *Barlow* fame played the psychopathic prisoner.

In the final episode, Tony Hoare's *The Long Good Thursday*, which went to air on 10 March 1994, Arthur receives a visit from an escaped prisoner who believes his wife is having an affair while he is serving his sentence. The escapee breaks into the lockup and holds Arthur hostage at gunpoint demanding that Arthur arrange for the wife to be brought there. When Arthur eventually placates the intruder and they leave the lockup together, the prisoner is recaptured and Arthur is arrested for harbouring an escaped prisoner. The episode closes with a magnificent aerial shot of a convoy of police vehicles crossing London's Albert Bridge taking Arthur, Ray and Dave into custody. Despite all his wrongdoings in the past, the audience cannot help feel a touch of sympathy for Arthur for taking the rap for something that was not of his doing.

This final episode has some interesting comparisons to the first. Without the humour and with less identifiable characters, the story could easily have filled a conventional drama spot. Like the first episode it deals with a captor and hostage situation. Secondly, like the first episode — and unlike most stories in the series, which are mainly slick and fast-moving — plenty of time is allowed, almost the entire middle third of the story, in which to develop and sustain the tension between Arthur and his captor. But in a reversal of roles, this episode sees the boss and not the minder pitted against the captor. And unlike the first episode, in which the hostage is finally seen as the hero, here we see the hostage arrested for harbouring a convicted criminal as he emerges from his ordeal.

Full circle

The week after the final episode went out, we saw George Cole dressed as his Arthur character, but appearing as himself, choosing a favourite episode. He chose the first, *Gunfight at the OK Laundrette*. Standards of political correctness and broadcasting acceptability had changed significantly over the programme's 14-year history, and ITV were forced to censor the original episode before they could rerun it. Racist remarks, blasphemy and a close-up shot of a stripper had to be removed before the episode was deemed suitable for re-broadcasting. In the original episode Arthur asks Terry how he could let himself be taken hostage by some 'dopey spades'. Managing director of

Central Broadcasting, Bob Southgate, vetted the programme before it went out. He said: 'The context of the story does not require them to be of any specific nationality and this kind of racial typecasting would be avoided by today's programme-makers.'[19]

Following the replay of the first episode, many critics and analysts drew attention to the way in which the show had gone full circle and catapulted the subordinate character to dominance. Max Davidson, in *The Daily Telegraph*, wrote:

> In its conception, George Cole's role was very much subordinate to Dennis Waterman's and amounted to little more than an engaging spiv, of the kind which Cole had played in dozens of instantly forgettable films. But just as Shakespeare's Falstaff came to dominate plays in which he had only been conceived as a second-ranking character, so Arthur Daley took on a life of his own and blossomed in a way that has passed into television folklore. It was a pity, although perhaps inevitable, that with the development of the character's comic possibilities, some of the series' other qualities suffered.[3]

Christopher Dunkley wrote in *The Financial Times:*[20]

> From the upbeat signature tune to the location filming of London, from the central importance of the tough Terry McCann character to the subordinate role played by George Cole's laughable Arthur Daley, this shrieks of what it actually was: an effort by the Thames TV subsidiary Euston Films to take the most notable aspects of *The Sweeney* and turn them into a vehicle for Dennis Waterman who had played the rough diamond sergeant in that police series. When you see in this first *Minder* episode armed police leaping from a Transit van, filmed from overhead, there is no mistaking the programme's antecedents.

> As time went by Waterman's limitations and Cole's strengths became clear, and the centre of gravity changed. Once McCann ceased to be the flywheel of the series there was less need for violent action and *Minder* became more a comedy of manners and character.[20]

Cast member Patrick Malahide highlighted the important role that Dennis Waterman had in sanctioning the change of emphasis:

> It actually started as a slam-bang action vehicle for Dennis as a follow-up to *The Sweeney*, but with him and George it just sort of grew into something else. And I think it's all credit to Dennis that he allowed that to happen. I don't think anybody really knew in the early days what it was we were making, and that's part of the magic, because it was allowed to grow organically.

Midway through season 8, after the minder had changed from Terry McCann to Ray Daley, Lewis Jones, in the *Daily Telegraph*, delivered a provocative analysis of the revamped programme under the headline 'Is *Minder* facing a Major change?'[21] The capitalisation of 'Major' was no coincidence. Jones's thesis was that Arthur was born out of the Thatcher era when times were hard. With a new prime minister in office: 'The new *Minder* reflects the changed conditions of Britain under the bland and kindly Mr Major'.

The old *Minder*, Jones pointed out, saw a distinct antipathy to police officers Chisholm and Rycott. The police were regarded as the enemy. 'But every week now Arthur seems to run to their replacements ... to beg for their help and protection.'

Jones was also apparently unimpressed with Ray Daley's ability to handle himself. 'The violence has taken on a decidedly cartoonish air,' he wrote. 'Ray is engagingly goofy but comparatively frail, not at all the kind cut out for the rough stuff.'

Max Davidson, in the *Daily Telegraph* three years later, had a similar view: 'Perhaps where *Minder* went off the rails was in trying to marry a wisecracking script to scenarios in which the threat of violence played an integral part — although, after the pleasure it gave for so long, it would take a brave man to complain'.[3]

An embodiment of the Thatcher era

Over its 14-year run, *Minder* became almost an embodiment of Thatcherism. Margaret Thatcher's contribution to *Minder's* success cannot be underestimated. As Malcolm Bradbury wrote in the *Daily Express*:

What really gave Arthur his long shelf life were the Thatcher Years. He became, even in his own mind, a classic entrepreneurial figure, and then Mr Business Opportunity doing his trilby-hatted best for Britain. When the summons of the Common Market came, Daley Enterprises even went into Europe.[22]

Arthur Daley's entrepreneurial idealism and his commitment to milk the system for whatever he could get out of it have become legendary. Even his name has entered the English language in its own right to describe someone of dubious financial integrity. When members of parliament refer in the House to a nation of Arthur Daleys, their meaning is entirely clear.

During the preparation of this book, George Cole was asked if he thought the programme would have achieved the same success if it had appeared five years later or five years earlier. He replied: 'I don't think five years earlier or later would have made any difference. It was the Thatcher years when greed was running high. We came into existence the same year Mrs T came to power. We outran her by four years.'

Patrick Malahide said: '*Minder* caught the mood of the age. There was something wonderfully subversive about it. I mean everybody hated Thatcher, and her Messianic brand of capitalism, and yet here was this dodgy character in a fawn overcoat rabbiting on about the wonders of free enterprise and getting it all wrong. It almost became a political satire. I honestly think *Minder* made people feel better about the eighties.'

A lovable rogue?

But maybe, just maybe, there was a down side. The Chief Constable of Cleveland, Christopher Payne, reportedly told a security seminar that juries were becoming more tolerant of petty criminals as a result of their portrayal on television as 'lovable rogues' such as Arthur Daley in *Minder* and Del Boy in *Only Fools and Horses*. Coincidentally, David Jason was named as BBC TV personality of the year in 1985 for his performance in *Only Fools and Horses* at the same awards ceremony in which George Cole and Dennis Waterman were named joint ITV personalities of the year for *Minder*.

The Chief Constable said: 'The central characters — regular receivers of stolen goods — are portrayed affectionately. Criminals are referred to cosily as a "Jack the Lad" while the stolen goods are merely "a bit iffy".[23] A panel member on the BBC-2 discussion programme *Did You See...?* also declared, in all seriousness, that Arthur Daley was 'an insidiously immoral invention, tending to corrupt public attitudes to petty crime'. Against this background, Lynne Truss in *The Times* considered that the term 'lovable rogue' is becoming a contradiction in terms.[4] But a lovable rogue Arthur undoubtedly was. Malcolm Bradbury, again:

> The British have always had a soft spot for the lovable rogue. For Arthur goes back to Shakespeare's Bardolph, Defoe's Moll Flanders and, of course, Dickens's Artful Dodger, and the Old Street ballads. They are always trying to beat the authorities, which is considered praiseworthy, but stop short of real evil. Such rogues become heroes because manipulating and cheating a hated social system is universally admired.[22]

In Arthur Daley's case, the admiration came also from the knowledge that he was one of us at heart, basically a sound chap. He had firm views on family, sex and religion. He was against violence (as written into the original character outline), and even when he was in a tight corner and called on his minder to 'Go on, hurt him, Terry!' we know we would have done the same if we were in the same position. Guns were a definite no no. Even his greed had a limit: he would never deal in drugs.

National icons

Against this sort of universal admiration, it was hardly surprising that the characters became firmly established as national icons. In September 1991, George Cole, as his Arthur Daley character, became the public face of the Leeds Building Society in the first of a series of popular television commercials. In May 1994, a few weeks after the final episode of *Minder* went to air, the Arthur Daley image graced the cover of *The Economist* as the personification of British entrepreneurship.

Even more unlikely, Arthur Daley and Terry McCann had earlier found their way into an educational video aimed at discouraging youngsters from using illicit drugs. A contributor to a *Minder* bulletin board on the Internet remembers the video from 1989 when he was at school. He wrote:

I remember Arthur in a cream suit at the start chatting to Dave in the Winchester. We weren't told it was an educational video so I assumed we were watching an episode I strangely hadn't seen before (I say strangely, as I had been a *Minder* fan from a very early age). Anyway, Arthur swiftly made an exit, I think he was off to Marbella! The rest of the film showed a young guy with no leisure pursuits who took drugs. In stark contrast, we were introduced to a certain Mr Terence McCann whose hobby of boxing kept him occupied in a healthy fashion.

The clear message was for kids to take up a sport to avoid getting into drugs. I remember at the time thinking Terence a slightly strange choice of role model for youngsters though! A drinker and womaniser who drove his ageing Capri too fast, kept dodgy company and never had a proper job! Actually, come to think of it, his lifestyle doesn't sound too bad at all!

A few years later, when Ray Daley was the minder, the role modelling was slightly more discreet. In *The Greatest Show in Willesden*, Ray says to his girlfriend, while discussing a possible business venture: 'Let me tell you something, Gloria. Me and Barry finished school in the same year. I left with two "O" levels. He left with the hubcaps off the caretaker's motor. Of course he's bloody dodgy.' The underlying message was not difficult to spot.

A gentleman star

Whatever role *Minder* had in the nation's psyche, probably the biggest contribution to the programme's success was George Cole's initial casting as Arthur Daley. Other artists were reportedly considered for the role, including the highly respected Denholm Elliott. But one can only surmise what *Minder* would have been without George Cole. It was not only his professionalism and experience as an actor, but his qualities as a person that made the character, and hence the show, what it was.

At the height of *Minder*'s success, Dennis Waterman told the *TV Times*:[24] 'Our relationship in *Minder* just seems to thrive, there's no professional jealousy between us at all.' He went on: 'I feel very fortunate working with someone like George.' In a later interview, he said: 'It sounds so showbizzy, but we had the best time you could have working. George and I laughed all day long. It was money for old rope, really.'[15]

In his autobiography *ReMinder*, Waterman writes: 'By the second episode we were brothers in arms, and woe betide any director who tried to get either of us to do anything we didn't agree with. I don't mean us to sound like a couple of prima donnas, who refused direction, but we both had exactly the same instinct about what worked and what didn't.'[12] George Cole echoed the sentiment: 'When we arrived at the production base in the morning we would go over any script changes we had marked overnight. Nearly always if one of us had marked a change the other would have marked the same thing.'

One other thing they fully agreed on was that the bad language should be toned down. Cole recollects that the decision was made in 1982 while he was working in *The Pirates of Penzance* at the Theatre Royal Drury Lane and Waterman was in *Windy City*. They noticed that there were always lots of youngsters who were fans of *Minder* outside the stage door asking for autographs. Cole recalls: 'We both agreed that the swearing had to go. The IBA (Independent Broadcasting Authority) were thrilled to bits about it.'

To a large extent it was the unique chemistry between Dennis Waterman and George Cole and their ability to ad-lib when the situation called for it that gave the programme its feel of spontaneity. As Glynn Edwards put it, 'The script was never a bible.' And Patrick Malahide: 'The scripts were stunning, but an awful lot was tweaked and refined on the day.'

George Cole said, 'Dennis and I understood each other so well that if one of us made a slip-up with his lines, the other one would invariably adjust his next line to correct it. We learned early on that one of the tricks when an ad-lib worked was to make the scriptwriters believe that we were saying what they had written. We were filming one episode in which Dennis was supposed to say, "Did you clock the geezer with the Panama hat?" But as he was about to say the line he looked around and realised that there wasn't anyone wearing a Panama hat. So instead he said, "Did you clock the geezer in the Wind in the Willows waistcoat?" And the line stayed in.'

Patrick Malahide said: 'I loved working with George Cole. He was such a gentleman. He would always be encouraging me to take the character further. A little quiet nod of the head and he'd whisper, 'Go on, go for it!' Remember that episode when Arthur was to appear as the foreman of the jury in a trial, and Chisholm was the prosecuting officer? Chisholm was outraged. I mean, beside himself and seething. It was George who made sure the director covered it properly. He could not have been more generous.

Gary Webster told the *TV Times:* 'I look at George and I think, "That's a career not of five minutes but of 50 years." I mean, it's easy to get started as I have but it's not easy to stay up there as he has. But George took me on board from the beginning, with no tension, no suggestion that there was this nervous young actor coming in who might ruin his scenes. He treated me like I'd been there for years.'[25]

Nicholas Day, who played Detective Sergeant Morley recalled: 'I have very fond memories of working on *Minder.* It was my favourite job in many years of work. George was hugely amusing and utterly professional.'

Glynn Edwards echoed the sentiment: 'George was a very quiet man, rather shy almost. There was none of this "Jack the Lad" attitude, laughing and carrying on with the crew. The job needs a lot of concentration and you have to keep the concentration going all the time. George would stay in his caravan studying the script and would come out for a couple of rehearsals and do the take and would go straight back to the caravan afterwards to prepare for the next scene. Sometimes at the end of the day we'd sit down with a lager from the Winchester's bar and have a chat about football or something but while we were working George stayed focused all the time. He was very professional.'

The last word

George Cole recalls: 'When we first started, our mobile home was a very old single-decker Green Line bus. It was a communal dressing room for all the cast and housed make-up and wardrobe. Once the series took off, Dennis and I were each given a palatial Winnebago [a luxury motor home]. That lasted one week. We spent so much time running back and forth discussing scenes we elected for one Winnebago which we shared. And that was the way it stayed. I don't think I have ever enjoyed working with anyone as much as I did with Dennis.'

Asked whether there were any episodes that he particularly enjoyed working on George Cole replied: 'With 107 episodes to choose from it is difficult to single out any particular one that I enjoyed more than any other, but I suppose the first *Minder* special, *Minder on the Orient Express*. It had a wonderful cast and we had twice as long to shoot it, 20 days instead of the usual ten.

'I suppose for my own safety I'd better mention the episode in which my wife, Penny Morrell, took part [Episode 62]. Arthur tried to fake his suicide in order to avoid the tax man. My wife played a hotelier who sheltered him thinking he was a famous writer who wanted to be incognito.'

Is there an episode that he was less happy to have worked on? He replied: 'I don't think so — apart from the one in which I had to be ducked in the Thames in midwinter!'

In November 1991, George Cole and Gary Webster were working at a studio in Islington, North London shooting a cover photograph for the Christmas edition of *TV Times*. Both were in Santa Claus outfits, Cole wearing his Arthur Daley trilby hat in place of a Santa hat. One of the crew called to George Cole that he had a telephone call in the office. 'There can't be,' he replied, 'Only my agent knows I'm here and she wouldn't have any reason to call me.' But the crew member was adamant that the call was for Cole. 'Take a message then and I'll call back,' instructed Cole. The assistant returned and announced, 'It's the Prime Minister's Office and they want to speak to you now.'

Cole recalls: 'I thought someone was playing some sort of joke. I said, "Well I can't walk through the building dressed like this. Tell them I'll call back later," which I did, and they told me I'd been nominated for an OBE.'

The award was announced in the New Year's Honours list for 1992, and was conferred by the Queen at Buckingham Palace on 26 March 1992. As George Cole said at the time, 'Arthur would probably have flogged it.'

References

1. 'The Real Arthur'. *TV Times* (London) 1991 Oct 26–Nov 1; p87.

2. Laurence, Charles. 'Why does the Jag cast a spell on our Arthur?' *The Sunday Telegraph* (London) 1989 Oct 1; p8.

3. Davidson, Max. 'The Arts: Nice little earner. Television Arthur Daley's first outing'. *The Daily Telegraph* (London) 1994 Mar 18; p22.

4. Armstrong, John Hurry. 'Obituary: Leon Griffiths'. *The Independent* (London) 1992 Jun 16; Sect: Gazette Page: p13.

5. Griffiths, Leon. *Minder.* New English Library: London, 1979.

6. 'Leon Griffiths'. *The Times* (London) 1992 Jun 12; Sect: Features.

7. Rieden, Juliet. 'This is the definitive Minder'. *TV Times* (London) 1994 Jan 15–21; p8.

8. White, Diane. 'You remember Rula, don't you? *The Boston Globe* 1989 Mar 8; Sect: Living: p65.

9. 'Brief Lives'. *The Sunday Times* (London) 1994 Mar 20; Sect: Features.

10. McDonald, James. 'Ducks to Peking — the variety that adds spice to Britain's export life'. *Financial Times* (London) 1984 Apr 21; Sect. I: p4.

11. Lawson, Mark. 'Television: Farewell to King Arfur'. *The Times* (London) 1985 Oct 5. ·

12. Waterman, Dennis. *ReMinder.* Arrow Books: London, 2000.

13. 'Obituary of Peter Childs'. *The Daily Telegraph* (London) 1989 Nov 1; Sect: Obituary: p23.

14. Truss, Lynne. 'Television workhorses finally put out to grass'. *The Times* (London) 1994 Mar 10; Sect: Features.

15. Smith, Dominic. 'TV heroes: 21) Dennis Waterman, Arthur Daley's sidekick Terry McCann in 80s hit *Minder'. Heat* 1999 Jun 26–Jul 2; p106.

16. 'Television: Feedback'. *The Independent* (London) 1991 Sept 11; Sect: Listings Page: p32.

17. Knight, Fiona. 'Day dream come true'. *TV Times* (London) 1991 Oct 12–18; p11.

18. 'Nice little earner killed off'. *The Times* (London) 1993 Oct 8; Sect: Home News.

19. Frean, Alexandra. 'TV censor tells Arthur to mind his language'. *The Times* (London) 1994 Mar 17; Sect. Home News.

20. Dunkley, Christopher. 'Farewell to a nice little era — Television'. *Financial Times* (London) 1994 Mar 16; Arts: p19.

21. Jones, Lewis. 'The Arts: Is "Minder" facing a Major change'. *The Daily Telegraph* (London) 1991 Oct 11; p17.

22. Bradbury, Malcolm. 'Requiem for a true rogue. So why do we love villains like Arthur Daley?' *Daily Mail* (London) 1993 Oct 9.

23. 'Attack on TV rogues'. *The Daily Telegraph* (London) 1989 May 12; p6.

24. 'It's been so good for them'. *TV Times* (London) 1984 Sep 7–13; p8.

25. Furness, Adrian. 'A nice little earner! George Cole taught me so much, says Minder Gary'. *TV Times* (London) 1993 Jan 2–8; p16.

What are they doing now?

George Cole

George Cole, OBE, lives just outside Henley-on-Thames with his wife Penny
Morrell in the house he had built in 1954 close to his mentor, the late Alastair
Sim. Despite celebrating his 77th birthday in April 2002, Cole has shown
little sign of slowing down since the final episode of *Minder* went to air.

He has had a number of notable stage roles, including a tour of Eric
Chappell's 1995 crime mystery *Theft*, (co-starring his wife, Penny Morrell), in
which he was cast in his familiar role as a lovable rogue, *Lock up your Daughters*

George Cole, 2002

in 1996, and Stephen Churchett's play *Heritage* in which he played a proud Chelsea pensioner.

Cole had a role in Julia Roberts' 1996 movie *Mary Reilly* playing the territorial butler and head of domestic staff in the household of Dr Jekyll and Mr Hyde. Recent television appearances include the title role in the 1997–99 series *Dad* as a mildly eccentric ageing widower, at odds with his son, and *Best of British* in 1999. He teamed up with Anna Massey in 2000 in the BBC's *The Sleeper* as the central characters, who lived a boring existence in a Devon rest home for elderly folk and set out to solve a mystery surrounding a friend of Massey's character.

At the time of writing he had just completed a five-part series for BBC radio based on Agatha Christie's Hercule Poirot stories, in which he plays Poirot's acquaintance, amateur detective Mr Satterthwaite. Will he ever retire? He said: 'You never really retire from acting. You know when it's time to stop when the work stops coming in.' Fortunately, this does not seem likely in the foreseeable future.

Dennis Waterman

In his autobiography *ReMinder*, published in 2000, Dennis Waterman describes the turbulent period in his private life post *Minder*: the increasingly acrimonious relationship with his wife Rula Lenska, huge debts after backing the failed movie *Cold Justice*, and eventually a financially crippling divorce settlement.

For a while he seemed to be concentrating on his stage work rather than television, touring in Britain and Australia, and doing the occasional Christmas pantomime. In 2001 he appeared in the movie *Arthur's Dyke* about four middle-aged friends who decide to repeat a 170-mile walk in Wales that they did years earlier as university students. Later that year he was cast as Alfred Dolittle in a highly successful stage revival of *My Fair Lady* in London's West End. His daughter Hannah has followed in his footsteps and now performs regularly in the BBC's *EastEnders*.

Gary Webster

Gary Webster is now married to television presenter Wendy Turner (from *Pet Rescue* on Channel 4) and they had a son in September 1999. They live in

Southwest London. Professionally, he has had a number of recent television appearances including the BBC-1 four-part drama serial *Real Women* in 1999 and guest roles in *My Wonderful Life* and *Doctors*. He is also a regular performer in Christmas pantomime, and it was here that he met his wife. She was playing Maid Marian in pantomime and he was Robin Hood.

Glynn Edwards

Now enjoying a well-deserved retirement, which he 'thoroughly recommends', Glynn Edwards lives happily with his wife, alternating their time between a country house in a small village in Spain, and, as a self-confessed 'boating nut' for 25 years, on a boat on the Mediterranean.

He still does the occasional guest appearance, 'when someone opens a new bar and wants a guest barman,' but most of the time he is happily pottering in the garden or on the boat and 'enjoying his wonderful grandchildren'.

Patrick Malahide

Patrick Malahide has made a number of telling appearances on the big screen in recent years, from the haughty ballet school principal in *Billy Elliott*, to a crooked Swiss banker in the Bond movie *The World is not Enough*. At the time of writing he is on stage at the National Theatre, playing the lead role in Sebastian Barry's *Hinterland*. He has a comprehensive website maintained by a loyal fan at *www.patrickmalahide.com*.

Nicholas Day

Nicholas Day has had an active and varied career on stage, film and television since his time as Detective Sergeant Morley in Seasons 8 and 9 of *Minder*. He has worked extensively at the National Theatre, most memorably in Patrick Marber's first play *Dealer's Choice* for which he created the role of Stephen, and most recently in *Tartuffe*. He has worked twice for the Royal Shakespeare Company, was with Kevin Spacey in the acclaimed *The Iceman Cometh* at the Almeids and Old Vic Theatres, and appeared most recently at the Royal Court in *Boy Gets Girl*. Since *Minder* he has also worked consistently in television programmes including *The Lakes, In Defence, A Great Deliverance, The*

Bill, Kavanagh QC, The Stretch and *Daniel Deronda.* Having recently played three policemen in a row he now seems to be embarked on a series of English Lords! He lives in London with his wife and daughter.

Peter Childs

Peter Childs appeared as Detective Sergeant Rycott in 15 episodes of *Minder* beginning with Episode 3 in 1979 and ending with Episode 72 in 1989. As mentioned in the main text, he died of leukaemia later in 1989. He was a hugely talented actor and had a string of stage and television appearances behind him. He was highly respected in his profession, and his premature death deprived us of an immensely accomplished performer.

Michael Povey

Michael Povey played Detective Constable Jones (later promoted to Detective Sergeant) in more than 20 episodes of *Minder* from 1982 to 1989. He is very active today in theatre in his native Wales.

Minder

The *Minder* series is still repeated occasionally on Independent Television in UK and has regular reruns on Granada Plus. It is still syndicated to many countries and recently had a successful revival on cable television in Australia. Occasional episodes have found their way onto VHS video over the years, the majority through the video distribution arm of Thames Television. With the demise of Thames Television, the videos went out of production and left very little available to the retail market.

In 2001, Clear Vision Video embarked upon a project to systematically release the entire series in chronological order for retail sale on VHS and DVD. At the time of writing (mid-2002) the company had released the first four seasons and expect to complete the remainder by 2005. A list of the titles currently available is given on page 69. Further information may be obtained from Clear Vision Ltd, PO Box 148, Enfield, Middlesex, EN3 4NR, England or by calling 020 8292 4875 or by visiting *www.clearvision.co.uk.*

A Minder *bibliography*

Books

Daley, Arthur (1994) *Back to Basics.* Heinemann. (hard cover)
  ISBN 0-434-00021-3
Daley, Arthur (narrator) (1994) *Back to Basics.* Random House Audiobooks
  ISBN 1-86021-908-X
Daley, Arthur (1995) *Back to Basics.* Mandarin. (paperback)
  ISBN 0-7493-1703-5
Daley, Arthur & Ableman, Paul (1991) *Straight Up.* (hard cover) Heineman
  ISBN 0-434-00066-3
Daley, Arthur & Ableman, Paul (1992) *Straight Up.* (paperback) Mandarin.
  ISBN 0-7493-1119-3
Griffiths, Leon (1979) *Minder.* New English Library (paperback)
  ISBN 0-450-04568-4
Griffiths, Leon (1985) *Arthur Daley's Guide to Doing it Right.* Collins (hard
  cover) ISBN 0-00-218176-2
Griffiths, Leon (1986) *Arthur Daley's Guide to Doing it Right.* Fontana
  (paperback) ISBN 0-00-637038-1
Masters, Anthony (1984) *Minder.* Sphere Books. (paperback)
  ISBN 0-7221-5824-6
Masters, Anthony (1984) *Minder — Back Again.* Sphere Books. (paperback)
  ISBN 0-7221-5823-8
Masters, Anthony (1985) *Minder — Back Again.* Severn House. (hard cover)
  ISBN 0-7278-1101-0
Masters, Anthony (1985) *Minder — Back Again.* Chivers. (hard cover, large
  print edition) ISBN 0-7451-0256-5
Masters, Anthony (1985) *Minder — Yet Again!* Sphere Books. (paperback)
  ISBN 0-7221-5827-0
Masters, Anthony (1985) *Minder.* Severn House. (hard cover)
  ISBN 0-7278-1021-9

Masters, Anthony (1985) *Minder.* Chivers. (hard cover, large print edition)
ISBN 0-7451-0208-5
Masters, Anthony (1986) *Minder — Yet Again!* Severn House. (hard cover)
ISBN 0-7278-1272-6
Minder Annual 1980. Grandreams. ISBN 0-86227-013-8
Minder Annual 1985. World International. ISBN 0-7235-6727-1
Minder Annual 1986. World International. ISBN 0-7235-6750-6
Waterman, Dennis (2000). *ReMinder.* Hutchinson. (hard cover)
ISBN 0-09-180108-7
Waterman, Dennis (2001). *ReMinder.* Arrow. (paperback) ISBN 0-09-928053-1

Internet resources

http://www.minder.org
An unofficial *Minder* fan club home page. Highly informative with a
bulletin board, chat line and links to music associated with the
programme.

http://www.geocities.com/arthurslockup/
An interesting and slightly esoteric site showing then-and-now views of
locations used in the *Minder* series.

http://www.users.zetnet.co.uk/itw/Thames/
A site giving an informative history of Thames Television.

http://www.uk.imdb.com
The International Movie Database. There is a useful search facility of
biographies of major film and television personalities, including artists
on *Minder.*

http://www.patrickmalahide.com
Patrick Malahide's home page. At the time of writing he is the only
principal artist on *Minder* to have a public home page.

http://www.clearvision.co.uk
Supplier of *Minder* DVDs and VHS tapes.

http://www.minderphenomenon.com
Home page for this book.

A Minder *videography*

Series	Part	Episodes	Date released	VHS No.	DVD No.
1	1	1–3	4/6/01	MDR001	MDRDVD001
1	2	4–6	4/6/01	MDR002	MDRDVD002
1	3	7–9	6/8/01	MDR003	MDRDVD003
1	4	10–11	6/8/01	MDR004	MDRDVD004
1	1–4	1–11	6/8/01	MBOX01	MBOXDVD01
2	1	12–14	8/10/01	MDR005	MDRDVD005
2	2	15–17	8/10/01	MDR006	MDRDVD006
2	3	18–20	8/10/01	MDR007	MDRDVD007
2	4	21–24	8/10/01	MDR008	MDRDVD008
2	1–4	12–24	8/10/01	MBOX02	MBOXDVD02
3	1	25–27	11/2/02	MDR009	MDRDVD009
3	2	28–30	11/2/02	MDR010	MDRDVD010
3	3	31–33	11/2/02	MDR011	MDRDVD011
3	4	34–37	11/2/02	MDR012	MDRDVD012
3	1–4	25–37	11/2/02	MBOX03	MBOXDVD03
4	1	39–41	10/6/02	MDR013	MDRDVD013
4	2	42–44	10/6/02	MDR014	MDRDVD014
4	3	45–47	10/6/02	MDR015	MDRDVD015
4	4	48–49	10/6/02	MDR016	MDRDVD016
4	1–4	39–49	10/6/02	MBOX04	MBOXDVD04
Minder specials		38, 58	7/10/02	MDR020	MDRDVD020
		65	14/1/02	CC8871	
		65	23/10/00		DED6037

All tapes/disks released by Clear Vision, except Episode 65, *Minder on the Orient Express*, released on VHS by Cinema Club and on DVD by Digital Entertainment Ltd.

Minder's slang

One of the factors that contributed to the enormous success of *Minder* over the years was its rich use of London slang and, in particular, cockney rhyming slang. This added a distinct atmosphere to the stories, which, combined with the ludicrous situations they depicted, provided a powerful form of escapism. It also allowed the bowler-hatted city gent from up-market Esher to go into the office the morning after a *Minder* episode and bandy about terms like 'boracic' and 'a nice looking kettle' as if they had been part of his vocabulary for years.

Although the television series was initially set in Fulham, in Southwest* London, Leon Griffith's initial film script, from which the television series evolved, was set in East London, where cockney slang had its origins and is still prevalent.

Arthur Daley, as a self-employed motor trader in Fulham and an erstwhile London street market trader, would certainly be expected to have a close familiarity with cockney slang, if not be a native speaker.

In fact, we have some difficulty in ascertaining Arthur's background. In one episode he talks about growing up during the war in East London. In another he talks of how he and Dave were members of the same gang when they were at school together in Brentford, which is in Northwest London.

Precise origins aside, Arthur Daley would have to be a cockney speaker for the *Minder* concept to be credible. So also would Terry McCann, his minder. In one episode Terry revisits his old school, which is right in the heart of cockney territory. And Arthur would probably not have been comfortable with a minder who was not a cockney. Whatever cockney language Terry might not have known, he would certainly have had a thorough coaching during his prison terms.

---

*   Postal designations involving the terms North London and South London do not, as many people think, have connotations related to north and south of the River Thames. The designations were traditionally assigned using Trafalgar Square as a reference point. Fulham, which has a Southwest London post-code, is north of the Thames. Londoners usually make distinctions related to the Thames with the terms 'south of the river' or 'north of the river'.

Origins

The word cockney comes from the Middle English *cokeney* meaning cock's egg, a term used to describe a misshapen egg from a young hen. The term was originally applied to simpletons and town-dwellers, who were perceived to be weaker than their country-dwelling counterparts. By the 17th century, the word took on a more specific pejorative sense meaning a Londoner.

The traditional definition of a cockney is a person born within the sound of Bow Bells, which are not in Bow at all, but are in the church of St Mary-le-Bow in Cheapside, in London EC2, dating back to 1091. In medieval times, Cheapside was London's main market place (*ceap* is Old English for market). Today it is a busy road running between St Pauls and Bank tube stations. In the 14th century, the Bow Bells used to ring out at nine o'clock each night to sound a curfew in London, which probably led to the notion that true cockneys were the only people who would be able to hear them (Weinreb and Hibbert, 1983).

Classification as a cockney, then, is technically on the basis of place of birth rather than use of a particular linguistic style. However, people are mobile and take their language with them when they move. It would take someone with exceptionally keen hearing to make out the sound of Bow Bells if they were just off Fulham High Street, where Arthur Daley had his first lockup. But many people in Fulham do undoubtedly speak in the same way as those in East London. For practical purposes, therefore, the term cockney is generally applied nowadays to Londoners who speak with the characteristic accent and use the unique terminology that has become known as cockney rhyming slang. But people born within the sound of Bow Bells still maintain a sense of pride that they really are *true* cockneys.

Cockney rhyming slang

Cockney rhyming slang originally came about as a way for the lower classes to engage in conversation without the upper classes, or those in authority, being able to understand. Many of the terms in use today have been around since the middle of the 19th century.

Typical rhyming slang consists of two or more words of which the second or last if more than two is the component that actually rhymes with the word that the term is used to represent. In most cases, only the first word of the slang term is used, the second part being understood. This helps preserve the exclusivity that the slang provides. Hence, few self-respecting cockneys would say, 'I came home a little bit elephant's trunk,' meaning drunk. They would simply say, 'I came home a little bit elephant's.' A few terms, however, are always used in their entirety, such as 'pen and ink' meaning 'stink'. It would be an unusual person indeed who says, 'There is a terrible pen in here.'

In the same way, no one who wanted to say, 'I would never believe it' would say, 'I would never Adam it.' It would always be 'Adam and Eve'. The skill in using cockney rhyming slang, therefore, lies not simply in knowing the vocabulary, but also in knowing which words are normally used together and which are normally broken up.

Some expressions only make sense in the context of the unique pronunciation of the cockney. 'Charing Cross', for 'horse', for example, does not work unless 'Cross' is pronounced to rhyme with 'horse', as a true cockney would. (He would also omit the final letter of 'Charing', but that is not relevant to the rhyme.) Similarly, 'baked potato' for 'waiter' makes absolutely no sense unless 'potato' is pronounced to rhyme with 'waiter' as it would be in East London.

Many of the terms that are used today are not traditional rhyming slang at all, but are recent constructions that have been contrived for entertainment. 'Ruby' for curry (after 1950s singer Ruby Murray) and 'Alans' for knickers (after television personality Alan Whicker) are fun at the time but will probably not have the same enduring quality as 'Barnet' for 'hair' (after Barnet Fair, a place in North London) or 'Hampsteads' for 'teeth' (after Hampstead Heath, also in London), both of which date to the mid-19th century.

One of Arthur Daley's oft-quoted expressions, 'Vera and philharmonic' for 'gin and tonic', was almost certainly created specially for comic effect in the show, although 'Vera' for 'gin' (after singer Vera Lynn) has been around since the end of World War II.

The glossary that follows is not restricted to rhyming slang. It is a selection of some of the general London slang terms that were used in the *Minder* series over the years, together, in many cases, with an indication of their origin. The list is by no means exhaustive and many well-known forms have been omitted. The examples of usage given are general ones and are not specifically taken from the *Minder* series. There are many comprehensive dictionaries of slang, and specifically London slang, available. Derivations given here have been verified in the sources listed below.

References

Ayto, John (2002) *The Oxford Dictionary of Rhyming Slang.* Oxford: Oxford University Press.

Franklyn, Julian (1975) *A Dictionary of Rhyming Slang.* London: Routledge.

Green, Jonathon (1998) *Cassell's Dictionary of Slang.* London: Cassell.

Partridge E. (1972) *The Penguin Dictionary of Historical Slang.* Abridged by J. Simpson. London: Penguin.

Partridge E. (1991) *A Concise Dictionary of Slang and Unconventional English.* Edited by P. Beale. London: Routledge.

Weinreb B, Hibbert C. (1983) *The London Encyclopaedia.* London: Macmillan.

Glossary

Abbreviations used
abbr. abbreviation of or for, abbreviated.
C. Century.
esp. especially

Ex. example of usage
r.s. rhyming slang

Adam and Eve. r.s. on *believe* (Ex. You'll never Adam and Eve who I just saw).

aeriated. excited or worked up; loss of composure, often due to anger. [possibly from *aeration* as in production of effervescence]

aris. abbr. r.s. from *Aristotle.* bottle. *q.v.* [usage known since 19th C.] Extension to bottle and glass. r.s. on *arse.*

bang to rights. retribution for one's crimes and misdemeanours (Ex. I've been waiting for weeks to catch you out and now I've got you bang to rights). ·

Barnet. abbr. r.s. from *Barnet Fair.* hair. [place in North London]

Bill. usually as *the Bill* or *the old Bill:* the police. [London cab driver's licence issued by Metropolitan Police since 1910 is known as the driver's bill]

bins. spectacles. [from *binoculars*]

bint. a girl or woman (usually in derogatory sense). [Arabic: daughter. *cf* Malay *binti:* used as part of female name to indicate daughter of]

bird. 1 young woman. 2 abbr. r.s. from *bird lime.* time, as in time spent serving a prison sentence (Ex. You'll probably get bird for that). Often preceded by *do* or *did* (Ex. I did most of my bird on the Moor). [*bird lime:* a viscous substance used to snare birds]

blag. theft (Ex. I was out blagging a place in Hampstead).

blagger. common thief; originally one who snatches a woman's handbag or commits robbery with force.

Bo Peep. r.s on *sleep.* [nursery rhyme character]

boat. abbr. r.s. from *boat race.* face.

bonce. head.

boob. 1 prison, cell. 2 usually as plural, female breasts.

book. to classify as (Ex. I wouldn't book him as a grass).

boracic. abbr. r.s. from *boracic lint.* skint *q.v.* short of or without money. [wound dressing impregnated with boric acid as an antiseptic]

bottle. abbr. r.s. from *bottle and glass.* arse. 1 bravery, courage (to lose one's bottle = to lose one's courage). 2 cheek, impertinence (Ex. I don't know how he's got the bottle to do that).

bovril, to lose one's. to lose one's courage. [Bovril: a foodstuff used to build up strength]

brace. two of something (Ex. A brace of lagers please barman).

Brahms and Liszt, often abbr. **Brahms.** r.s. on *pissed.* drunk. [composers of classical music, usage dates to 1920s]

brass. prostitute. abbr. of *brass nail* [usage known from 1920s, origin uncertain]

brief. 1 lawyer. 2 ticket for football match etc. [German: letter, document]

bristols. (always as plural) abbr. r.s. from *Bristol City,* hence *titty.* female breasts. [a football team in SW England]

brown bread. r.s. on *dead.*

bubble. abbr. r.s. from *bubble and squeak.* a Greek. [type of food]

bull and cow. r.s. on *row.* argument, disturbance, quarrel.

bunce. money [dates from mid-20th C., origin unclear, possibly from *bonus*]

bung. 1 gratuity, tip, bribe, present (Ex. He'll do it but he'll need a bung). Occasionally used with *throw* or *chuck* (Ex. I'll need to chuck him a bung). 2 throw, toss, put in position (Ex. Bung those boxes down over there).

bunny. excessive talk or chatter [see **rabbit** *q.v.*]

bury the hobnail. kick (usually a person during a fight). [from hobnail boots]

butcher's. abbr. r.s. from *butcher's hook*. look (Ex. Come and have a butcher's at this).

carsey. see **kahsi**

case. watch or observe a property prior to commission of a criminal act esp. as in *case the joint.*

Chalfonts. abbr. r.s. from *Chalfont St Giles.* piles i.e. haemorrhoids [place in Buckinghamshire north of London]

china. abbr. r.s. from *china plate*. mate.

chuffed. delighted, pleased with.

clobber. 1 miscellaneous encumbrances and impedimenta esp. when travelling (Ex. Do we really have to take all that clobber with us?). [probably from Yiddish: old clothes, usage known from mid 19th C.] 2 punch, strike, assault (Ex. I'll clobber him if he doesn't shut up).

clock. see or notice something (Ex. Did you clock what sort of car it was?).

cobblers. abbr. r.s. from *cobbler's awls.* 1 balls, as in testicles. 2 nonsense, worthless talk (Ex. I don't want to hear any of that cobblers). [from awl — tool used by a shoemaker]

cockle. abbr. r.s. from *cock and hen*. ten, hence ten pounds.

codgell. handouts of leftover produce from workers at Covent Garden fruit and vegetable market. [presumably mispronunciation of **cotchel** *q.v.*]

collar. steal, take (Ex. His boss collars 10 percent of the takings). *have one's collar felt:* get arrested or detained by the police (Ex. I nearly got my collar felt this afternoon).

con[1]. 1 abbr. for *confidence trick* (Ex. They've got a good con going). 2 swindle, deceive (Ex. Be careful they don't con you out of your winnings).

con[2]. abbr. convict.

con man, con artist. confidence tricksters.

cop[1]. 1 catch, receive, or take hold of something that is thrown (Ex. Cop hold of this). 2 look at or take notice of (Ex. Did you cop the view from the window?).

cop[2]. 1 police officer. 2 capture or arrest (as in *a fair cop*).

cotchel. *Oxford English Dictionary* defines as 'a portion (of grain, etc.) left in a sack or bag; a small remnant of a larger quantity.' [usage in this context known from mid-19th C. *cf* **codgell**]

cream. beat or severely injure a person esp. during a fight, smash to pulp esp. in a figurative sense (Ex. The driver was creamed in the accident).

crumpet. women in general but esp. as sex objects (Ex. I'll see if I can pick up a bit of crumpet at the disco).

crust. 1 income to support existence (Ex. That's the only honest crust you'll ever earn). 2 a living (in sense of livelihood) (Ex. We've all got to earn a crust).

cut. a share of the proceeds.

daisies. abbr. r.s. from *daisy roots*. boots. [usage known from 1874]

dead ringer of or **for.** an exact copy of, hard to tell the difference from; a fake that looks realistic.

do over. 1 assault (Ex. If he does that again we'll do him over). 2 rob premises (Ex. They are planning to do the place over tomorrow night).

doddle. easy task (Ex. That safe will be a doddle to open).

dodgy. awkward, unreliable, cunning, tricky, artful, suspicious.

dog. abbr. r.s. from *dog and bone*. telephone.

dough. money.

down to. on account of, due to, the responsibility of (Ex. All this damage is down to you).

drift. intention or meaning, direction or line of thought.

drink. payment of money, usually a small amount, as a gratuity or tip for a service (Ex. There's a drink in it for you when the job is finished). **on a drink**. in expectation of a tip or gratuity.

drum. house, home, residence, business property (Ex. I thought he could stay at your drum for a couple of days).

duff up. assault.

Duke of York. r.s. on *chalk* (rarely, if ever, abbreviated).

ear, out on one's. ignominiously or humiliatingly ejected, removed, or disbarred from a place.

earner. project or activity which attracts a profit.

earwig. eavesdrop, listen in on, hence **earwigging**.

elbow in (occasionally followed by *on*). Obtain access forcibly. **elbow out**. remove. **give** someone **the elbow**. send away, dismiss, reject.

elephant's. abbr. r.s. from *elephant's trunk*. drunk.

fence. one who buys and sells stolen property. act of buying and selling stolen property.

filth. police.

flash. given to showing off or acting in a conspicuous or conceited way.

flog. sell.

flyover, propping up a. murdered with no trace of the body [from act of disposing of body in mixed concrete which will be used in construction of elevated highway]

form. prison record.

frame, in the. suspected of having committed some form of offence.

front. 1 cheek, impertinence (Ex. He's got a lot of front to try that in front of a copper). 2 lend or advance money (Ex. Could you front me a couple of quid until the end of the week). **up front**. in advance of or before work, deal, etc. commences (Ex. Fifty quid up front and the rest when the job is finished). **front up**. make an appearance.

gaff. home, residence, or business property.

gaffer. foreman, boss, person in charge.

game, on the. involved in prostitution or thieving.

g.b.h. abbr. *grievous bodily harm*. severe injuries caused as result of violent assault. Often used as hyperbole (g.b.h. of the ear holes = incessant talking).

geezer. a person esp. an old man.

git. a worthless person (Ex. Look at that stupid git across the road).

goner, gonner. a dead body (Ex. I don't want to end up a goner).

Gordon Bennett! A mild expletive [James Gordon Bennett 1795–1892: founder of *New York Herald* newspaper]

governor usually pronounced as 'guv'nor'. 1 one's employer 2 one's superior officer in police force.

graft. work. **grafter**. worker, hence grafted, grafting (Ex. He really grafted yesterday = worked hard).

grand. thousand. usually applied to money ex. fifty grand = £50,000.

grass. abbr. r.s. on *grasshopper*. copper, hence police informer, give information to the police or authorities, thence **grassed**, **grassing**.

green. inexperienced, naïve, gullible.

greenstuff occasionally preceded by *folding*. banknotes.

Gregory. abbr. r.s. from *Gregory Peck*. 1 neck. 2 cheque. [after American film actor]

guv. abbr. **governor** *q.v.* a form of address esp. as applied to one perceived to be superior.

half inch. r.s. on *pinch*. steal.

Hampsteads. abbr. r.s. from *Hampstead Heath*. teeth. [place in North London]

hard nut. tough, fearless person.

have it away. run away, abscond.

heavy mob. the police (usually of senior rank or specialist group ex. Fraud Squad).

hook, sling one's. take one's leave, go away (Ex. Why don't you just sling your hook?).

hookey. stolen, dishonest, or acquired dishonestly.

Hooray. abbr. Hooray Henry. rich ineffectual young man.

hooter. nose.

hump. carry (Ex. I'll just hump these boxes
round to the van).

hump, got the. angry, emotionally upset.

iffy. doubtful, uncertain, attracting suspicion.

inside. in prison.

Irish. abbr. r.s. from *Irish jig.* wig.

iron. abbr. r.s. from *iron hoof* on poof.
homosexual.

jack it in. cease or stop an activity (Ex. I'm
going to jack it in for the night).

Jack and Jill. r.s on *money till.* [nursery rhyme
characters]

Jack the lad. a person given to behaving in a
conspicuous or conceited way (Ex. He's
always trying to be Jack the lad).

Jam tart. r.s. on *heart.*

Jimmy. abbr. r.s. from *Jimmy Riddle.* piddle,
i.e. pass urine.

Jock. Scotsman.

joy. success, satisfaction (Ex. You won't get
much joy out of him).

kahsi, karsi (also **carsey**). toilet. [origins
uncertain, probably from 19th C. *case:* water
closet, or *casa:* isolated room, brothel]

keen. good quality, pleasing (Ex. He plays a
keen game of snooker).

kettle. abbr. r.s. from *kettle and hob.* a watch
(after fob watch but applies to watches
generally). [originally thieves' slang from
early 19th C.: a red kettle = a gold watch,
a tin kettle = a silver watch; rhyme
probably added later]

kettle of fish (usually preceded by *a nice, a
pretty, a right,* etc). muddle, confusion,
upheaval (Ex. That's a right kettle of fish
and no mistake). [from Scottish: kettle of
fish = picnic, usage known from 19th C.]

kibosh on, put the. put an end to (Ex. That
put the kibosh on their little game).
[probably from Yiddish: *kabas, kabbasten:* to
suppress]

kip. sleep (Ex. I'll go and have a couple of
hours' kip).

kipper. make appear stupid (Ex. They did
me up like a kipper).

kite. blank or worthless cheque. [from 1920s:
fly a kite = pass a worthless cheque]

knock. 1 cheat (Ex. Why would I want to
knock you for the price of a drink?). 2
speak badly or disparagingly about (Ex.
I'm not going to listen to you knocking
my mate like that). **knock out** sell or
dispose of (Ex. I'm knocking them out at
fifty pounds a piece).

kosher. correct; legitimate; proper; genuine
[Hebrew: proper]

lardy. abbr. r.s. from *la-di-dah.* cigar. Stuck up,
conceited. [usage known from early 20th
C.]

leak. act of passing urine (Ex. I'm going out
for a leak). Have (or take) a leak. Urinate.

leg it. run off (Ex. As soon as we hear the
bell we'll leg it).

leg over. sexual intercourse or to engage in
such, hence: get one's leg over.

legit. abbr. legitimate, honest.

lemon¹. acrimonious, caustic, etc. form of
speech or behaviour (Ex. Don't try to get
lemon with me).

lemon². stupid person or one easily taken
advantage of (Ex. Don't all rush off and
leave me standing here like a lemon).

lemonade. black person. r.s. on **spade.** *q.v.*

lift. steal.

Lily Law. the police. [esp. used by London
barrow boys since 1930s]

Lucozade. black person. r.s. on **spade.** *q.v.*
[tonic drink]

manor. 1 district served by a particular police
station. 2 the immediate vicinity (Ex. I've
never heard of anyone with that name on
this manor).

mark (someone's) card. to provide someone
with information about; to tip off [bar-
row boy's slang since around 1945, from
racecard: programme of events at horse
race meeting]

merchant banker. r.s. on *wanker.*

minces. abbr. r.s. from mince pies. Eyes.
[usage known from late 19th C.]

moby. abbr. r.s. from *Moby Dick.* 1 nick *q.v.* (as in prison) 2 sick (to be ill) [fictitious whale]

mockers on, put the. 1 bring bad luck to. 2 put a stop to (Ex. That's put the mockers on the horse running next week). [Yiddish]

monkey. five hundred pounds. [decoration on 500 Rupee note during time of British Raj *cf* **pony** *q.v.*]

monkey's, I don't give a. I don't care about.

mons (pronounced monze). 1 (often followed by *it up*) to spoil (something) (Ex. We know what we're doing now so don't mons it up this time). 2 a disaster, bad outcome (Ex. It was a right mons from start to finish). [historical slang for female genitalia, probably from *mons Veneris*]

moosh. derogatory form of address to a man (Ex. Here moosh, what do you think you're doing?). [Gypsy origin]

moriarty. r.s. on *party* [character in Sherlock Holmes stories]

mouse. moustache.

mug up. study. Also **mug up on.**

muscle. 1 strong or muscular person, often hired to give protection (Ex. You're not the only muscle around here). 2 muscular force or exertion of bodily strength, esp. by fighting (Ex. I throw a bit of muscle around).

mutton. abbr. r.s. from *Mutt and Jeff.* deaf. [popular name for war medals from World War I, later used as names of comic characters]

nawse, norse. abbr. *nausea, nauseate, nauseous* 1 (often followed by *it up*) to spoil (something) (Ex. Everything is working well so don't go and nawse it up). 2 a disaster, bad outcome (Ex. It turned into a complete nawse when the other lot arrived). [British forces slang from mid-20th C.]

neck, save one's. protect one's security or best interests.

needle. 1 fit of bad temper (Ex. He's got the dead needle with you). 2 irritate (Ex. Are you trying to needle me?).

Nelson Eddy's. occasionally just **Nelson.** r.s. on *readies q.v.* ready money [usage dates from 1980s after name of actor/singer]

nick. 1 condition (Ex. His car looks in pretty good nick for the price). 2 prison, police station. 3 police arrest (Ex. He's bound to get nicked if he keeps on like that). 4 steal. 5 go nimbly or quickly (Ex. Nick out the back way while nobody's looking).

ninepence in the shilling. of low intellect; poor ability to reason. [from pre-decimal currency in UK (ninepence was three-quarters the value of a shilling), hence, usage as *not the full amount.*]

ninepence, as right as. fit, well, in good form.

north and south. r.s. on *mouth.*

nuts. testicles.

Old King Cole. r.s. on *dole.* unemployment benefit. [nursery rhyme character, usage dates from 1920s]

oppo. colleague or friend. [from *opposite number*]

other, a bit of the. sexual intercourse.

owe. be under obligation to a person (differs from normal usage in that the nature of what is owed is not specified) (Ex. He owes me [i.e. a favour, service or repayment, etc.]).

pad. living quarters, place of residence or lodging.

Paddy. Irishman.

Peckham. abbr. r.s. from *Peckham Rye.* necktie [place in South London]

pen and ink. r.s. on *stink;* smell badly (Ex. There's a terrible pen and ink in here).

penny stamp. r.s. on *tramp.*

peter. abbr. r.s. from *Peter Dell.* prison cell, safe (as in a store for valuables). [origin uncertain]

pillock. stupid person, a fool.

pins. legs (rarely if ever used in singular).

piss, take the. make fun of, often followed by *out of.*

piss artist. one who acts in a conceited or pretentious way.

piss off. take leave or go away (often used as imperative) (Ex. Just piss off and leave us alone!).

pissed off. unhappy, annoyed.

plates. abbr. r.s. from *plates of meat.* feet.

Plod. the police. [from Mr Plod, a policeman in childrens' literature]

plonker. penis esp. as *pull one's plonker* = to make fun of or play a joke on someone [usage known from 1917]

plot. immediate vicinity. *cf* **manor** *q.v.*

pocket, in someone's. easy to manipulate, esp. as result of a bribe (Ex. I've got him well in my pocket).

poncing about. behaving in an affected, unusual or contrived way.

pony. twenty five pounds. [decoration on 25 Rupee note during time of British Raj *cf* **monkey** *q.v.*]

porkies. abbr. r.s. from *pork pies.* lies (as in untruths).

porridge. prison sentence.

poxy. of poor quality, worthless, worthy of contempt (Ex. The poxy car was not worth the money we paid for it). [from *pox*, old term for syphilis]

prat. mild pejorative (Ex. Now what's the stupid prat up to?). [originally a term for female genital area, usage known from 19th C.]

puke. vomit.

pull. act of arresting or detaining a person by the police.

punt. tout or solicit potential customers or clients for something.

punter. customer or client.

purse. profit, payment resulting from a successful outcome [boxing term: *purse* the prize money in a boxing match]

QT, on the. quietly, secretly, surreptitiously.

quid. pound in British currency.

rabbit. abbr. r.s. from *rabbit and pork.* talk (excessively or pointlessly), hence also **bunny** *q.v.*.

radio rental. r.s. on *mental.* crazy or insane [name of electrical rental company in Britain]

readies. (always used in plural) banknotes, ready money.

real McCoy. the genuine article.

Richard. abbr. r.s. from *Richard the Third.* **bird** *q.v.* a young woman. [usage known from late 19th C.]

ricket. a mistake.

right hander. punch with the fist of the right hand.

ringer. 1 person who changes the appearance of a stolen car in preparation for resale. 2 a car so altered. *q.v.* **dead ringer of.**

rip-off. 1 a fraud, swindle or scheme to do so. 2 financial exploitation (Ex. Fifty pounds is a bit of a rip-off isn't it?).

Roller. Rolls-Royce car.

ropey. of poor quality. [probably derived from 'made of rope rather than wool']

rub-a-dub. r.s. on *pub* [nursery rhyme]

ruck. abbr. ruckus. 1 heated argument, commotion. 2 brawl, gang fight.

run-around, give the. be deceitful or evasive.

runner, do a. run off or run away.

sad. of poor or disappointing quality.

scarper. run away.

schlep (schlepped, schlepping). 1 carry, drag. 2 to put somewhere (Ex. Schlep it down in the corner). 3 move or travel laboriously (Ex. I've spent the day schlepping down from Manchester). [Yiddish]

schmalzer. one given to expressing undue sweetness or excessive praise. [German *Schmalz:* dripping or lard, hence connotation of oiliness]

schmock. 1 disagreeable person. 2 a fool. [originally from German *Schmuck:* ornament, adopted by Yiddish: penis]

schmutter. clothing material, clothes in general esp. a suit. [Yiddish]

schtook (also shtook). trouble.

schwartzer. black person. [German *schwarz:* black]

score to settle. amends to be made (Ex. I've got a score to settle with you about that car you sold me).

screw. prison officer.

scum bag. worthless or despicable person.

septic. abbr. r.s. on *septic tank.* Yank. An American.

set up. put in a dangerous or vulnerable position (Ex. I think I've been set up).

set-up. 1 dangerous, unexpected, disadvantageous or vulnerable position created deliberately (Ex. This must be a set-up). 2 an arrangement or organisation (Ex. That was a nice little set-up that George was running).

Sexton. abbr. r.s. from *Sexton Blake.* fake. [character in crime fiction stories. Usage known from mid-20th C.]

shooter. gun, firearm.

shop. give information to police or authorities.

shove it! imperative: Stop it!

shovel. abbr. r.s. from *shovel and broom.* room. (hence usage as *prison* or more specifically *prison cell*).

sight for sore eyes. unexpected or welcome sight.

skint. short of or without money. [from *skinned* past participle of *skin*]

skive. evade work, responsibility, duty, etc; occasionally followed by *off* (Ex. I don't want you to skive off while we're not here).

sky. abbr. r.s. from *sky rocket.* pocket. [usage known from 1879]

slag. 1 despicable person. 2 prostitute, promiscuous woman. 3 often followed by *off.* criticise, insult, make disparaging comments about.

slate, on the. on account, a debt to be paid later.

slaughter. place of residence [originally a secluded place where thieves etc. would transfer or trade stolen property, probably from *slaughter yard,* i.e. a place which is generally avoided by other people]

snappy. neat and elegant.

snide. false, counterfeit, bogus, esp. currency.

sod. 1 unpleasant or awkward person or thing (Ex. That silly sod standing with his back to us). 2 a specific person, often in jocular sense or as term of endearment (Ex. The old sod is really quite sweet). **sod all.** nothing (Ex. There is sod all left). **sodding.** a mild pejorative expressing antipathy, annoyance or extreme condition (Ex. It was a sodding great thing). [from Sodomite, originally coarse pejorative pre-19th C.; abbreviated to current form early 19th C.]

solitary. abbr. *solitary confinement.* isolation from other prisoners.

sov. abbr. *sovereign.* old gold coin worth one pound, hence 200 sovs = £200.

s.p. important or essential information (Ex. I've got the s.p. on you = I know all about you). [horse-racing term: abbr. for *starting price* as in the odds at which a horse starts a race, and hence the important information]

spade. black person (usage known from around 1920). [from colour of the card suit, as in 'as black as the ace of spades']

St Louis'. abbr. r.s. from *St Louis Blues.* shoes. [after musical tune]

stand in. allocate a share or make a contribution towards something (Ex. Stand me in for 10 pounds).

stitch up. betray or cheat.

stretch. prison sentence, usually preceded by measure of time (Ex. A three-month stretch).

stripe. defraud.

stroppy. abbr. obstreperous. [usage known from mid-20th C.]

stumm. quiet, refrain from disclosing information, etc. Also **keep stumm**), as imperative: keep quiet! [German *stumm:* dumb, mute]

sunbeam, sunshine. form of address, often derogatory or to demonstrate that recipient is perceived as of inferior status (Ex. Listen sunbeam, I don't want any trouble).

sus, suss. 1 understand, work out, realise. Often followed by out (Ex. We sussed you out with no trouble). 2 investigate, inspect (Ex. I need to go and sus out a bit of business).

syrup. abbr. r.s. from *Syrup of Fig.* wig. [proprietary pharmaceutical product]

tart. wife, girlfriend or woman in general (often as term of endearment). [differs from other usage in that there is no implication that person referred to is a prostitute]

tea leaf. r.s on *thief.*

tenner. ten pounds.

thin on the ground. of little substance, not convincing.

throw. per unit (Ex. They are letting them go at 15 quid a throw). [originally fairground term]

throw up. vomit.

ticker. 1 the heart (Ex. He's having a bit of trouble with his ticker). 2 accountant.

tickle. 1 robbery, burglary or proceeds thereof. 2 successful result generating a small reward.

tight-fisted. stingy, careful or mean with money.

titfer. abbr. r.s. from *tit for tat.* hat.

tod, on one's. on one's own. abbr. r.s. from *Tod Sloan.* own. [late Victorian jockey]

toe rag, tow rag. despicable, worthless person. [authorities are divided over whether the term originates from the strips of cloth that convicts and tramps wrapped around their feet as a substitute for socks or a worthless piece of rag tied on a tow rope to indicate that a vessel or vehicle is being towed]

tom. abbr. r.s. from *tomfoolery.* jewellery.

tom tit. r.s. on *shit.* [species of bird]

ton. one hundred pounds sterling.

ton of [hot] bricks, come down on like a. give a severe punishment or reprimand to a person (Ex. If I find you doing that again I'll come down on you like a ton of bricks).

top. kill, execute. **top one's self.** commit suicide.

trombone. r.s. on *telephone.*

trumpet. telephone.

turn over. 1 commit burglary. 2 cheat or swindle. 3 (police slang) conduct a search of premises. 4 (prison slang) cell search [from turning over of mattress to ensure nothing is concealed underneath]

twig. notice, realise (Ex. I didn't twig that he was a copper).

two and eight. r.s. on *state.* condition (Ex. They were in a right old two and eight when we got there). [British pre-decimal currency: two shillings and eightpence, usage known since World War I]

Uncle Dick. r.s. on *sick.* unwell.

V.A.T. abbr. 1 value added tax. 2 vodka and tonic.

VAT man. collector of value added tax.

Vera. abbr. r.s. from *Vera Lynn.* gin. [after Vera Lynn, British female singer during and after World War II]

Vera *q.v.* **and philharmonic.** r.s. on *gin and tonic.*

villain. 1 rogue, rascal (usually jocular). 2 one who commits offences (often of petty nature). 3 anyone with a criminal record.

wally. stupid person; a fool. (mild pejorative) [*wally* is a name given to a small cucumber pickled in brine and resembling a small penis, originally used synonymously with *prick* to denote a contemptuous person]

wedge. money esp. as in a wad or stack of banknotes. Occasionally **lump of wedge.**

weigh in with. to add something that was not there earlier (Ex. As soon as the others pay up I'll weigh in with my share). [from sporting term applied to weighing of jockey after a horse race or a boxer before a bout]

wheels. car, vehicle. (get me some wheels = get me a car); **wheels man.** car driver (esp. expert driver or car driver during commission of a crime).

whistle. abbr. r.s. from *whistle and flute.* suit (of clothes).

wimp. weak, feeble or ineffectual person.

wind up[1]. (rhymes with 'lined up') joke or trick pulled on a person (Ex. If I didn't know better I'd think it was a wind up). Also **on a wind up**. play a joke or trick on a person (Ex. Are you trying to wind me up?). [as in winding a spring or clockwork mechanism and waiting to see the effect]

wind up[2]. (rhymes with 'pinned up') esp. **get** or **had the wind up**. a fright (Ex. He really got the wind up when he thought the police were on to him).

woofter. r.s. from *poofter.* homosexual.

wrong 'n. person with a dishonest or criminal attitude or background.

Index of key characters and situations

Chronological episode list

Minder *episodes in order of first UK transmission date.*

	SEASON 1	
1	*Gunfight at the OK Laundrette* by Leon Griffiths	29/10/79
2	*Bury My Half at Waltham Green* by Paul Wheeler	5/11/79
3	*The Smaller They Are* by Leon Griffiths	12/11/79
4	*A Tethered Goat* by Murray Smith	19/11/79
5	*The Bounty Hunter* by Bernie Cooper and Francis Megahy	26/11/79
6	*Aces High — and Sometimes Very Low* by Leon Griffiths	3/12/79
7	*The Bengal Tiger* by Leon Griffiths	10/12/79
8	*Come in T-64, Your Time is Ticking Away* by Tony Hoare	17/12/79
9	*Monday Night Fever* by Leon Griffiths	7/1/80
10	*The Dessert Song* by Andrew Payne	14/1/80
11	*You Gotta Have Friends* by Leon Griffiths	21/1/80

	SEASON 2	
12	*National Pelmet* by Willis Hall	11/9/80
13	*Whose Wife is it Anyway* by Tony Hoare	18/9/80
14	*You Lose Some, You Win Some* by Jeremy Burnham	25/9/80
15	*Don't Tell Them Willie Boy Was Here* by Paul Wheeler	9/10/80
16	*Not a Bad Lad, Dad* by Tony Hoare	16/10/80
17	*The Beer Hunter* by Willis Hall	23/10/80
18	*A Nice Little Wine* by Stanley Price	30/10/80
19	*All Mod Cons* by Andrew Payne	6/11/80
20	*Diamonds are a Girl's Worst Enemy* by Paul Wheeler	20/11/80
21	*The Old School Tie* by Jeremy Burnham	27/11/80
22	*All About Scoring, Innit* by Willis Hall	4/12/80
23	*Caught in the Act, Fact* by Tony Hoare	11/12/80
24	*A Lot of Bull and a Pat on the Back* by Tony Hoare	18/12/80

SEASON 3

25	*Dead Men Do Tell Tales* by Tony Hoare	13/1/82
26	*You Need Hands* by Andrew Payne	20/1/82
27	*Rembrandt Doesn't Live Here Anymore* by Dave Humphries	27/1/82
28	*Looking for Micky* by Tony Hoare	3/2/82
29	*Dreamhouse* by Andrew Payne	10/2/82
30	*Another Bride, Another Groom* by Willis Hall	17/2/82
31	*The Birdman of Wormwood Scrubs* by Leon Griffiths	24/2/82
32	*The Son Also Rises* by Paul Wheeler	3/10/82
33	*Why Pay Tax* by Leon Griffiths	10/3/82
34	*Broken Arrow* by George Day	17/3/82
35	*Poetic Justice, Innit?* by Tony Hoare	24/3/82
36	*Back in Good Old England* by Andrew Payne	31/3/82
37	*In* by Leon Griffiths	7/4/82

SEASON 4

38	*Minder's Christmas Bonus* by Leon Griffiths	26/12/83
39	*Rocky Eight and a Half* by Leon Griffiths	11/1/84
40	*Senior Citizen Caine* by Andrew Payne	18/1/84
41	*High Drains Pilferer* by Dave Humphries	25/1/84
42	*Sorry Pal, Wrong Number* by Leon Griffiths	1/2/84
43	*The Car Lot Baggers* by Trevor Preston	8/2/84
44	*If Money be the Food of Love, Play on* by Tony Hoare	15/2/84
45	*A Star is Gorn* by Tony Hoare	22/2/84
46	*Willesden Suite* by Andrew Payne	29/2/84
47	*Windows* by Geoff Case	7/3/84
48	*Get Daley!* by Andrew Payne	14/3/84
49	*A Well Fashioned Fit-up* by Barry Purchese	21/3/84

SEASON 5

50	*Goodbye Sailor* by Andrew Payne	5/9/84
51	*What Makes Shamy Run?* by Leon Griffiths	12/9/84
52	*A Number of Old Wives' Tales* by Tony Hoare	19/9/84
53	*The Second Time Around* by Geoffrey Case	26/9/84
54	*Second Hand Pose* by Tony Hoare	10/10/84
55	*The Long Ride Back to Scratchwood* by Leon Griffiths	17/10/84*
56	*Hypnotising Rita* by Alan James	24/10/84*
57	*The Balance of Power* by David Yallop	31/10/84*
58	*Around the Corner* by Tony Hoare	26/12/84

SEASON 6

59	*Give Us This Day Arthur Daley's Bread* by Andrew Payne	4/9/85
60	*Life in the Fast Food Lane* by Alistair Beaton	11/9/85
61	*The Return of the Invincible Man* by Leon Griffiths	18/9/85
62	*Arthur is Dead, Long Live Arthur* by Tony Hoare	25/10/85
63	*From Fulham with Love* by Tony Hoare	2/10/85
64	*Waiting for Goddard* by Leon Griffiths	9/10/85

CHRISTMAS SPECIALS

| 65 | *Minder on the Orient Express* by Andrew Payne | 25/12/85 |
| 66 | *An Officer and a Car Salesman* by Tony Hoare | 26/12/88 |

SEASON 7

67	*It's a Sorry Lorry, Morrie* by Tony Hoare	2/1/89
68	*Days of Fines and Closures* by David Yallop	9/1/89
69	*Fatal Impression* by Anita Bronson	16/1/89
70	*The Last Video Show* by Andrew Payne	23/1/89
71	*Fiddler on the Hoof* by David Humphries	30/1/89
72	*The Wrong Goodbye* by David Yallop	6/2/89

---

* Transmission of episodes 55, 56, and 57 was disrupted by an ITV industrial dispute. The dates shown above for these episodes are the intended transmission dates. The actual transmission dates of episodes 55 and 56 varied from region to region. Episode 57 was shown in all regions on 1 January 1985.

SEASON 8

73	*The Loneliness of the Long Distance Entrepreneur* by David A. Yallop	5/9/91
74	*A Bouquet of Barbed Wine* by Kevin Sperring and Bernard Dempsey	12/9/91
75	*Whatever Happened to Her Indoors* by David A.Yallop	19/9/91
76	*Three Cons Make a Mountain* by David A. Yallop	26/9/91
77	*Guess Who's Coming to Pinner* by David A. Yallop	3/10/91
78	*The Last Temptation of Daley* by William Ivory	10/10/91
79	*A Bird in the Hand is Worth Two in Shepherd's Bush* by David A. Yallop	17/10/91
80	*Him Indoors* by Iain Roy and Chris Kelly	24/10/91
81	*The Greatest Show in Willesden* by Kevin Sperring and Bernard Dempsey	31/10/91
82	*Too Many Crooks* by Tony Jordan	7/11/91
83	*The Odds Couple* by Tony Jordan and Liane Aukin	14/11/91
84	*The Coach That Came in from the Cold* by Kevin Clark	21/11/91
85	*The Cruel Canal* by Kevin Sperring and Bernard Dempsey	25/12/91

SEASON 9

86	*I'll Never Forget Whats 'Ername* by William Ivory	7/1/93
87	*No Way to Treat a Daley* by Tim Firth	14/1/93
88	*Uneasy Rider* by Geoff Rowley	21/1/93
89	*Looking for Mr. Goodtime* by David A. Yallop	28/1/93
90	*Opportunity Knocks and Bruises* by Chris Kelly and Iain Roy	4/2/93
91	*Gone with the Winchester* by Bernard Dempsey and Kevin Sperring	11/2/93
92	*How to Succeed in Business Without Really Retiring* by William Ivory	18/2/93
93	*The Roof of All Evil* by William Ivory	25/2/93
94	*Last Orders at the Winchester* by Gary Lawson and John Phelps	4/3/93
95	*Cars and Pints and Pains* by David A. Yallop	11/3/93
96	*The Great Trilby* by Bernard Dempsey and Kevin Sperring	18/3/93
97	*A Taste of Money* by William Ivory	25/3/93
98	*For a Few Dollars More* by Bernard Dempsey and Kevin Sperring	1/4/93

SEASON 10

99	*A Fridge Too Far* by Bernard Dempsey and Kevin Sperring	6/1/94
100	*Another Case of Van Blank* by William Ivory	13/1/94
101	*All Things Brighton Beautiful* by Tony Hoare	20/1/94
102	*One Flew Over the Parents' Nest* by Tony Hoare	27/1/94
103	*The Immaculate Contraption* by William Ivory	3/2/94
104	*All Quiet on the West End Front* by Bernard Dempsey and Kevin Sperring	10/2/94
105	*The Great Depression of 1994* by Arthur Ellis	17/2/94
106	*On the Autofront* by William Ivory	24/2/94
107	*Bring Me the Head of Arthur Daley* by Bernard Dempsey and Kevin Sperring	3/3/94
108	*The Long Good Thursday* by Tony Hoare	10/3/94

Alphabetical episode list

Minder *episode titles and numbers alphabetically.*

Artists' index

Performing artists by episode number; names listed as credited.

Price, Annabel 55
Price, Stanley 16
Prockter, Colin 23, 68
Quatro, Suzy 25
Quick, Diana 66
Quilligan, Denis 81
Quince, Peter 44, 71
Quinn, Patricia 27
Rabett, Catherine 47
Raggett, Nick 87
Raistrick, George 94
Ramone, Monica 27
Rapley, John 37
Rashleigh, Andy 82
Ratcliff, Sandy 29
Rattray, Iain 40, 66
Rawle, Jeff 88
Raynsford, Gary 66
Rea, Charles 56
Rea, Stephen 47
Read, Bunny 49
Read, Darryl 8
Read, Martyn 74
Reader, Phillip 75
Reddin, Jacqueline 51
Redfern, Michael 56
Redford, Ian 69
Reding, Nick 79
Redwood, Manning 65
Rees, Anwen 69
Regan, Linda 1
Reid, Beryl 53
Reid, Mike 26
Reith, Douglas 19
Reynolds, Paul 99
Reynolds, Stephen 101
Richards, Angela 40
Richards, Gavin 94
Ridings, Richard 87
Ringham, John 20
Ripper, Michael 57
Ritchie, Joe 31

Ritchie, June 5
Ritchie, Vivienne 52
Roach, Pat 61
Robbins, Michael 19
Robert, Jeffrey 89
Roberts, Ivor 53
Roberts, Norman 106
Robertson, Margaret 84
Robins, Toby 46
Robinson, Tony 102
Roe, Charlie 74
Rogers, Charles 31
Rogers, Mitzi 22
Rogers, Tania 15
Roles, Natalie 90
Rolfe, John 23
Rose, Clifford 57
Ross, Adlyn 96
Ross, Willie 79
Rossiter, Pat 96
Roughley, Lill 73, 75, 79, 86, 91, 102
Rourke, William 17
Rouse, Simon 80
Rovai, Daniel 65
Rowe, Alan 89
Rowe, John 46, 77
Rowley, Nikola 22
Rowley, Troy 98
Roza, Debbie 71
Rozelaar-Green, Frank 79
Rubin, Dot 53
Ruby, Thelma 68
Ruskin, Sheila 41
Rutherford, Peter 50
Rutland, John 81
Rutter, Barrie 17
Ryall David 76
Ryan, Hilary 3
Ryecart, Patrick 70
Sachs, Andrew 101
Sachs, Hugh 87
Salaman, Chloe 43

Writers' index

Script writers by episode and transmission date; names listed as credited.

WRITER	TITLE	EPISODE	DATE
Beaton, Alistair	*Life in the Fast Food Lane*	60	11/09/85
Bronson, Anita	*Fatal Impression*	69	16/01/89
Burnham, Jeremy	*The Old School Tie*	21	27/11/80
Burnham, Jeremy	*You Lose Some, You Win Some*	14	25/09/80
Case, Geoff	*Windows*	47	7/03/84
Case, Geoffrey	*The Second Time Around*	53	26/09/84
Clark, Kevin	*The Coach That Came in from the Cold*	84	21/11/91
Cooper & Megahy†	*The Bounty Hunter*	5	26/11/79
Day, George	*Broken Arrow*	34	17/03/82
Dempsey & Sperring†	*All Quiet on the West End Front*	104	10/02/94
Dempsey & Sperring†	*A Fridge Too Far*	99	6/01/94
Dempsey & Sperring†	*Bring Me the Head of Arthur Daley*	107	3/03/94
Dempsey & Sperring†	*For a Few Dollars More*	98	1/04/93
Dempsey & Sperring†	*Gone With the Winchester*	91	11/02/93
Dempsey & Sperring†	*The Great Trilby*	96	18/03/93
Ellis, Arthur	*The Great Depression of 1994*	105	17/02/94
Firth, Tim	*No Way to Treat a Daley*	87	14/01/93
Griffiths, Leon	*Aces High — and Sometimes Very Low*	6	3/12/79
Griffiths, Leon	*Gunfight at the OK Laundrette*	1	29/10/79
Griffiths, Leon	*In*	37	7/04/82
Griffiths, Leon	*Minder's Christmas Bonus*	38	26/12/83
Griffiths, Leon	*Monday Night Fever*	9	7/01/80
Griffiths, Leon	*Rocky Eight and a Half*	39	11/01/84
Griffiths, Leon	*Sorry Pal, Wrong Number*	42	1/02/84
Griffiths, Leon	*The Bengal Tiger*	7	10/12/79
Griffiths, Leon	*The Birdman of Wormwood Scrubs*	31	24/02/82
Griffiths, Leon	*The Long Ride Back to Scratchwood*	55	17/10/84*
Griffiths, Leon	*The Return of the Invincible Man*	61	18/09/85

WRITER	TITLE	EPISODE	DATE
Griffiths, Leon	*The Smaller They Are*	3	12/11/79
Griffiths, Leon	*Waiting for Goddard*	64	9/10/85
Griffiths, Leon	*What Makes Shamy Run?*	51	12/09/84
Griffiths, Leon	*Why Pay Tax*	33	10/03/82
Griffiths, Leon	*You Gotta Have Friends*	11	21/01/80
Hall, Willis	*All About Scoring, Innit*	22	4/12/80
Hall, Willis	*Another Bride, Another Groom*	30	17/02/82
Hall, Willis	*National Pelmet*	12	11/09/80
Hall, Willis	*The Beer Hunter*	17	23/10/80
Hoare, Tony	*A Lot of Bull and a Pat on the Back*	24	18/12/80
Hoare, Tony	*A Number of Old Wives' Tales*	52	19/09/84
Hoare, Tony	*A Star is Gorn*	45	22/02/84
Hoare, Tony	*An Officer and a Car Salesman*	66	26/12/88
Hoare, Tony	*Around the Corner*	58	26/12/84
Hoare, Tony	*Arthur is Dead, Long Live Arthur*	62	25/10/85
Hoare, Tony	*Caught in the Act, Fact*	23	11/12/80
Hoare, Tony	*Come in T-64, Your Time is Ticking Away*	8	17/12/79
Hoare, Tony	*Dead Men Do Tell Tales*	25	13/01/82
Hoare, Tony	*From Fulham with Love*	63	2/10/85
Hoare, Tony	*If Money Be the Food of Love, Play On*	44	15/02/84
Hoare, Tony	*It's a Sorry Lorry, Morrie*	67	2/01/89
Hoare, Tony	*Looking for Micky*	28	3/02/82
Hoare, Tony	*Not a Bad Lad, Dad*	16	16/10/80
Hoare, Tony	*Poetic Justice, Innit?*	35	24/03/82
Hoare, Tony	*Second Hand Pose*	54	10/10/84
Hoare, Tony	*Whose Wife is it Anyway*	13	18/09/80
Hoare, Tony	*All Things Brighton Beautiful*	101	20/01/94
Hoare, Tony	*One Flew Over the Parents' Nest*	102	27/01/94
Hoare, Tony	*The Long Good Thursday*	108	10/03/94
Humphries, Dave	*High Drains Pilferer*	41	25/01/84
Humphries, Dave	*Rembrandt Doesn't Live Here Anymore*	27	27/01/82
Humphries, David	*Fiddler on the Hoof*	71	30/01/89
Ivory, William	*A Taste of Money*	97	25/03/93
Ivory, William	*Another Case of Van Blank*	100	13/01/94
Ivory, William	*How to Succeed in Business Without Really Retiring*	92	19/02/93
Ivory, William	*I'll Never Forget Whats 'Ername*	86	7/01/93
Ivory, William	*On the Autofront*	106	24/02/94

WRITER	TITLE	EPISODE	DATE
Ivory, William	*The Immaculate Contraption*	103	3/02/94
Ivory, William	*The Last Temptation of Daley*	78	10/10/91
Ivory, William	*The Roof of All Evil*	93	25/02/93
James, Alan	*Hypnotising Rita*	56	24/10/84*
Jordan & Aukin†	*The Odds Couple*	83	14/11/91
Jordan, Tony	*Too Many Crooks*	82	7/11/91
Kelly, Chris & Roy, Iain	*Opportunity Knocks and Bruises*	90	4/02/93
Lawson & Phelps†	*Last Orders at the Winchester*	94	4/03/93
Payne, Andrew	*All Mod Cons*	19	6/11/80
Payne, Andrew	*Back in Good Old England*	36	31/03/82
Payne, Andrew	*Dreamhouse*	29	10/02/82
Payne, Andrew	*Get Daley!*	48	14/03/84
Payne, Andrew	*Give Us This Day Arthur Daley's Bread*	59	4/09/85
Payne, Andrew	*Goodbye Sailor*	50	5/09/84
Payne, Andrew	*Minder on the Orient Express*	65	25/12/85
Payne, Andrew	*Senior Citizen Caine*	40	18/01/84
Payne, Andrew	*The Dessert Song*	10	14/01/80
Payne, Andrew	*The Last Video Show*	70	23/01/89
Payne, Andrew	*Willesden Suite*	46	29/02/84
Payne, Andrew	*You Need Hands*	26	20/01/82
Preston, Trevor	*The Car Lot Baggers*	43	8/02/84
Price, Stanley	*A Nice Little Wine*	18	30/10/80
Purchese, Barry	*A Well Fashioned Fit-up*	49	21/03/84
Rowley, Geoff	*Uneasy Rider*	88	21/01/93
Roy, Iain & Kelly, Chris	*Him Indoors*	80	24/10/91
Smith Murray	*A Tethered Goat*	4	19/11/79
Sperring & Dempsey†	*A Bouquet of Barbed Wine*	74	12/09/91
Sperring & Dempsey†	*The Cruel Canal*	85	25/12/91
Sperring & Dempsey†	*The Greatest Show in Willesden*	81	31/10/91
Wheeler, Paul	*Bury My Half at Waltham Green*	2	5/11/79
Wheeler, Paul	*Diamonds are a Girl's Worst Enemy*	20	20/11/80
Wheeler, Paul	*Don't Tell Them Willie Boy Was Here*	15	9/10/80
Wheeler, Paul	*The Son Also Rises*	32	3/03/82
Yallop, David	*Days of Fines and Closures*	68	9/01/89
Yallop, David	*The Balance of Power*	57	31/10/84*
Yallop, David	*The Wrong Goodbye*	72	6/02/89
Yallop, David A.	*Three Cons Make a Mountain*	76	26/09/91
Yallop, David A.	*Whatever Happened to Her Indoors*	75	19/09/91

WRITER	TITLE	EPISODE	DATE
Yallop, David A.	*A Bird in the Hand is Worth Two in Shepherd's Bush*	79	17/10/91
Yallop, David A.	*Cars and Pints and Pains*	95	11/03/93
Yallop, David A.	*Guess Who's Coming to Pinner*	77	3/10/91
Yallop, David A.	*Looking for Mr. Goodtime*	89	28/01/93
Yallop, David A.	*The Loneliness of the Long Distance Entrepreneur*	73	5/09/91

†   *Abbreviated names*
    Cooper & Megahy = Cooper, Bernie & Megahy, Francis
    Dempsey & Sperring = Dempsey, Bernard & Sperring, Kevin
    Jordan & Aukin = Jordan, Tony & Liane Aukin
    Lawson & Phelps = Lawson, Gary & Phelps, John
    Sperring & Dempsey = Sperring, Kevin & Dempsey, Bernard

*   Transmission of episodes 55, 56, and 57 was disrupted by an ITV industrial dispute. The dates shown above for these episodes are the intended transmission dates. The actual transmission dates of episodes 55 and 56 varied from region to region. Episode 57 was shown in all regions on 1 January 1985.

Directors' index

Directors by episode and transmission date.

DIRECTOR	TITLE	EPISODE	DATE
Abey, Dennis	*Don't Tell Them Willie Boy Was Here*	15	9/10/80
Bamford, Roger	*A Bird in the Hand is Worth Two in Shepherd's Bush*	79	17/10/91
Bamford, Roger	*A Taste of Money*	97	25/3/93
Bamford, Roger	*For a Few Dollars More*	98	1/4/93
Bamford, Roger	*Him Indoors*	80	24/10/91
Bamford, Roger	*The Great Trilby*	96	18/3/93
Bamford, Roger	*Whatever Happened to Her Indoors*	75	19/9/91
Banham, Derek	*The Greatest Show in Willesden*	81	31/10/91
Beeson, Charles	*A Fridge Too Far*	99	6/1/94
Brayne, William	*Days of Fines and Closures*	68	9/1/89
Campbell, Martin	*All About Scoring, Innit*	22	4/12/80
Campbell, Martin	*National Pelmet*	12	11/9/80
Clegg, Tom	*Looking for Micky*	28	3/2/82
Clegg, Tom	*The Beer Hunter*	17	23/10/80
Clegg, Tom	*Dreamhouse*	29	10/2/82
Clegg, Tom	*Rembrandt Doesn't Live Here Anymore*	27	27/1/82
Flemyng, Gordon	*All Things Brighton Beautiful*	101	20/1/94
Flemyng, Gordon	*Looking for Mr. Goodtime*	89	28/1/93
Flemyng, Gordon	*The Great Depression of 1994*	105	17/2/94
Flemyng, Gordon	*The Immaculate Contraption*	103	3/2/94
Flemyng, Gordon	*The Roof of All Evil*	93	25/2/93
Gatward, James	*A Tethered Goat*	4	19/11/79
Gatward, James	*The Old School Tie*	21	27/11/80
Gatward, James	*You Lose Some, You Win Some*	14	25/9/80
Gordon Clark, Lawrence	*Cars and Pints and Pains*	95	11/3/93
Gordon Clark, Lawrence	*I'll Never Forget What's 'Ername*	86	7/1/93
Gordon Clark, Lawrence	*No Way to Treat a Daley*	87	14/1/93

DIRECTOR	TITLE	EPISODE	DATE
Gordon Clark, Lawrence	*The Long Good Thursday*	108	10/3/94
Gordon Clark, Lawrence	*Gone With the Winchester*	91	11/2/93
Green, Terry	*A Lot of Bull and a Pat on the Back*	24	18/12/80
Green, Terry	*Arthur is Dead, Long Live Arthur*	62	25/10/85
Green, Terry	*Caught in the Act, Fact*	23	11/12/80
Green, Terry	*Hypnotising Rita*	56	24/10/84*
Green, Terry	*If Money be the Food of Love, Play on*	44	15/2/84
Green, Terry	*Poetic Justice, Innit?*	35	24/3/82
Green, Terry	*Fatal Impression*	69	16/1/89
Green, Terry	*Fiddler on the Hoof*	71	30/1/89
Green, Terry	*Life in the Fast Food Lane*	60	11/9/85
Green, Terry	*Sorry Pal, Wrong Number*	42	1/2/84
Green, Terry	*The Long Ride Back to Scratchwood*	55	17/10/84*
Green, Terry	*What Makes Shamy Run?*	51	12/9/84
Hallum, Alister	*Too Many Crooks*	82	7/11/91
Hannam, Ken	*Another Case of Van Blank*	100	13/1/94
Hill, Jim	*A Well Fashioned Fit-up*	49	21/3/84
King, Chris	*Diamonds are a Girl's Worst Enemy*	20	20/11/80
King, Christopher	*Bury My Half at Waltham Green*	2	5/11/79
Lawrence, Diarmuid	*A Bouquet of Barbed Wine*	74	12/9/91
Lawrence, Diarmuid	*All Quiet on the West End Front*	104	10/2/94
Lawrence, Diarmuid	*Guess Who's Coming to Pinner*	77	3/10/91
Lawrence, Diarmuid	*Opportunity Knocks and Bruises*	90	4/2/93
Lawrence, Diarmuid	*The Last Temptation of Daley*	78	10/10/91
Lawrence, Diarmuid	*The Loneliness of the Long Distance Entrepreneur*	73	5/9/91
Lawrence, Diarmuid	*Uneasy Rider*	88	21/1/93
Megahy, Francis	*A Number of Old Wives' Tales*	52	19/9/84
Megahy, Francis	*Come in T-64, Your Time is Ticking Away*	8	17/12/79
Megahy, Francis	*From Fulham with Love*	63	2/10/85
Megahy, Francis	*The Son Also Rises*	32	3/3/82
Megahy, Francis	*Back in Good Old England*	36	31/3/82
Megahy, Francis	*Give Us This Day Arthur Daley's Bread*	59	4/9/85
Megahy, Francis	*Goodbye Sailor*	50	5/9/84
Megahy, Francis	*Minder on the Orient Express*	65	25/12/85
Megahy, Francis	*The Balance of Power*	57	31/10/84*
Megahy, Francis	*The Car Lot Baggers*	43	8/2/84
Megahy, Francis	*The Second Time Around*	53	26/9/84

DIRECTOR	TITLE	EPISODE	DATE
Megahy, Francis	*The Wrong Goodbye*	72	6/2/89
Megahy, Francis	*Willesden Suite*	46	29/2/84
Menaul, Chris	*A Nice Little Wine*	18	30/10/80
Quinn, AJ	*Last Orders at the Winchester*	94	4/3/93
Reardon, John	*One Flew Over the Parents' Nest*	102	27/1/94
Sasdy, Peter	*Gunfight at the OK Laundrette*	1	29/1079
Sasdy, Peter	*The Bounty Hunter*	5	26/11/79
Sasdy, Peter	*The Bengal Tiger*	7	10/12/79
Sharp, Ian	*All Mod Cons*	19	6/11/80
Sharp, Ian	*You Need Hands*	26	20/1/82
Standeven, Richard	*How to Succeed in Business Without Really Retiring*	92	19/2/93
Standeven, Richard	*The Coach That Came in from the Cold*	84	21/11/91
Stroud, John	*Bring Me the Head of Arthur Daley*	107	3/3/94
Taylor, Baz	*On the Autofront*	106	24/2/94
Toynton, Ian	*A Star is Gorn*	45	22/2/84
Toynton, Ian	*Not a Bad Lad, Dad*	16	16/10/80
Toynton, Ian	*Get Daley!*	48	14/3/84
Toynton, Ian	*In*	37	7/4/82
Toynton, Ian	*Minder's Christmas Bonus*	38	26/12/83
Toynton, Ian	*Rocky Eight and a Half*	39	11/1/84
Toynton, Ian	*The Birdman of Wormwood Scrubs*	31	24/2/82
Toynton, Ian	*You Gotta Have Friends*	11	21/1/80
Vardy, Mike	*Three Cons Make a Mountain*	76	26/9/91
Vardy, Mike	*Another Bride, Another Groom*	30	17/2/82
Vardy, Mike	*Monday Night Fever*	9	7/1/80
Ward Baker, Roy	*Aces High — and Sometimes Very Low*	6	3/12/79
Ward Baker, Roy	*An Officer and a Car Salesman*	66	26/12/88
Ward Baker, Roy	*Around the Corner*	58	26/12/84
Ward Baker, Roy	*Broken Arrow*	34	17/3/82
Ward Baker, Roy	*It's a Sorry Lorry, Morrie*	67	2/1/89
Ward Baker, Roy	*Second Hand Pose*	54	10/10/84
Ward Baker, Roy	*The Dessert Song*	10	14/1/80
Ward Baker, Roy	*The Last Video Show*	70	23/1/89
Ward Baker, Roy	*The Return of the Invincible Man*	61	18/9/85
Ward Baker, Roy	*The Smaller They Are*	3	12/11/79
Ward Baker, Roy	*Waiting for Goddard*	64	9/10/85
Ward Baker, Roy	*Whose Wife is it Anyway*	13	18/9/80

DIRECTOR	TITLE	EPISODE	DATE
Ward Baker, Roy	*Why Pay Tax*	33	10/3/82
Washington, Keith	*The Odds Couple*	83	14/11/91
Washington, Keith	*The Cruel Canal*	85	25/12/91
Young, Robert	*Senior Citizen Caine*	40	18/1/84
Young, Robert	*Dead Men Do Tell Tales*	25	13/1/82
Young, Robert	*Windows*	47	7/3/84
Young, Robert	*High Drains Pilferer*	41	25/1/84

* Transmission of episodes 55, 56, and 57 was disrupted by an ITV industrial dispute. The dates shown above for these episodes are the intended transmission dates. The actual transmission dates of episodes 55 and 56 varied from region to region. Episode 57 was shown in all regions on 1 January 1985.

Episode guide

Episode 1

Season 1/1   First transmission: 29 October 1979

Gunfight at the OK Laundrette
by Leon Griffiths

Terry . . . . Dennis Waterman	*Stretch* . . . . .Trevor Thomas
Arthur . . . . .George Cole	*Winston* . . . . William Vanderpuye
Dave . . . . Glynn Edwards	*Chief Superintendent* . . . . .Donald Burton
Alfie . . . . Dave King	*Chisholm* . . . . Patrick Malahide
Irishman . . . . Tony Doyle	*DC Harney* . . . . David Killick
Liz . . . . Linda Regan	
Bernie . . . . .Arnold Diamond	Producers . . .Lloyd Shirley, George Taylor
Cosmo . . . . Leroi Samuels	Director . . . . .Peter Sasdy
Mrs Mayhew . . . . Hilary Mason	Executive Producer . . .Verity Lambert

This first episode is a perfectly credible hostage drama with some humour added on. Terry accompanies Arthur's old friend Alfie to empty the cash machines at his launderette business while his regular bodyguard is away getting married. While they are working in one of the shops they find themselves at the centre of an armed hold-up in which Alfie is shot and injured and they are both taken as hostages along with an elderly woman customer. As time passes we see the strong interplay between Terry and Stretch, the ringleader, and the fear of the two youngsters he has recruited to help. This eventually leads to hopelessness for Stretch as he realises there is no way out. The question might easily be asked why the police Chief Superintendent handles the case personally (and so badly) without calling in a hostage negotiator, especially when he is told that the incident is political. The humour, which adds little to the story, comes from Arthur's attempts to profit from the situation by selling the story to the press.

Episode 2

Season 1/2   First transmission: 5 November 1979

Bury My Half at Waltham Green
by Paul Wheeler

Terry . . . . .Dennis Waterman	*Albert Stubbs* . . . . .Kenneth Cope
Arthur . . . . George Cole	
Italian client . . . . .not credited	
Rose . . . . Ann Lynn	Producers . . Lloyd Shirley, George Taylor
Jack . . . . Tony Selby	Director . . . . Christopher King
George . . . . Nicky Henson	Executive Producer . . . Verity Lambert

Arthur assigns Terry to mind Albert Stubbs for a few days on his release from a prison sentence for bank robbery. Stubbs buried the £50,000 proceeds of the robbery in a field before his arrest and intends to recover it and leave the country while the rest of the gang are still in prison. Rose Mellors, the wife of one of the other gang members, also wants to get her hands on the proceeds, and she and her minder Jack track down Stubbs in Terry's flat. Terry has to come up with a plan to satisfy all the interested parties.

Episode 3

First transmission: 12 November 1979·

The Smaller They Are
by Leon Griffiths

Terry . . . . Dennis Waterman		*Eric* . . . . Chris Jenkinson	
Arthur . . . . .George Cole		*Hotel manager* . . . . .Michael Segal	
Big Stan . . . . David Jackson		*Pub landlord* . . . . George Tovey	
Dave . . . . Glynn Edwards		*Airline receptionist* . . . . Hilary Ryan	
Scotch Harry . . . . .Phil McCall			
Brian . . . . Osmund Bullock			
Kim . . . . Susan Vanner		Producers . . .Lloyd Shirley, George Taylor	
Rycott . . . . Peter Childs		Director . . . . Roy Ward Baker	
Maurice Bonnet . . . . .Hans Meyer		Executive Producer . . .Verity Lambert	

Arthur changes an American $100 note as a favour for Big Stan and discovers that Stan's pal Scotch Harry has another half-million dollars in a briefcase he snatched at the air terminal. Worried that the owner of the money will track them down, Arthur persuades Scotch Harry to return the money to its owner — in exchange for a generous commission that Arthur will negotiate. But they soon discover that they are dealing with a nasty group of international currency smugglers. They also find that that DC Rycott also has an interest in returning the case to its owner.

This is the first episode in which Arthur uses the term 'er indoors to refer to his wife. When Arthur and Terry see an attractive young girl at a pub bar Arthur says, 'See, that's what 'er indoors don't understand. A young bird like that hanging round keeps yer feeling young.' To which Terry replies, 'I thought it was Phyllosan and Grecian 2000.'

Episode 4

Season 1/4

First transmission: 19 November 1979

A Tethered Goat
by Murray Smith

Terry	.............Dennis Waterman	*Asif*	.... Mohamed Sultan
Arthur	.... George Cole	*First police sergeant*	..........Ian Collier
George	.............Johnny Shannon	*Second police sergeant*	.......David Millet
Elliot	..............Michael Sheard	*Police inspector*	..........Patrick Jordan
Sardi	..............Nadim Sawalha		
Bassam Sayin	..........Lee Montague	Producers	.. Lloyd Shirley, George Taylor
Dai Llewellyn	........Kenneth Griffith	Director	.... James Gatward
Frankie	...........Jenny Lee-Wright	Executive Producer	... Verity Lambert

Terry has to mind Mr Sayin, an Arab banker from Lebanon, who is worried because Terry doesn't carry a gun. Terry's suspicions that Sayin is in danger are confirmed when armed intruders break into the safe house that Arthur has rented for Sayin. Terry moves to another hideout with Sayin and Dai Llewellyn, the Welsh manservant whom Arthur has supplied to attend on the Arab. The gang put pressure on Arthur to reveal the location of Sayid's hideout. Arthur is never more pleased to see the police.

Episode 5

Season 1/5   First transmission: 26 November 1979

The Bounty Hunter
by Bernie Cooper and Francis Megahy

Terry . . . . Dennis Waterman	*Fenton* . . . . .Derek Jacobi
Arthur . . . . .George Cole	*Garage attendant* . . . . Paul Satvender
Des . . . . .George Layton	*Val* . . . . Rikki Howard
Harold . . . . .Christopher Biggins	*John* . . . . Peter Dean
Jo . . . . June Ritchie	*Andy* . . . . .Keith Alexander
Shopkeeper . . . . Brian Godfrey	
Graham Hurst . . . . .James Aubrey	Producers . . .Lloyd Shirley, George Taylor
Ralph Hurst . . . . Tony Steedman	Director . . . . .Peter Sasdy
Mrs Hurst . . . . Kathleen Byron	Executive Producer . . .Verity Lambert

Jo, a young widow, has been cheated out of her late husband's insurance payment in a Majorcan property scam. Arthur offers Terry's help to try to recover her money. Terry tracks down Freddie Fenton who masterminded the scam, but he claims to have no money and refuses to offer any compensation — until Terry's pal Des relieves him of his Rolls-Royce.

This is the first of six appearances of George Layton in the programme as Des, a dubious motor mechanic, and the first time Terry's white Capri seen in the opening titles also appears in an episode. There is also an impressive stunt in which Terry jumps off a bridge onto a waiting lorry.

Subplots: Terry finds himself unknowingly assisting Des in the theft of luxury cars, and Arthur wants to join a select gambling club.

Episode 6

Season 1/6   First transmission: 3 December 1979

Aces High — and Sometimes Very Low
by Leon Griffiths

Terry . . . . .Dennis Waterman	*George* . . . . Andreas Markos
Arthur . . . . George Cole	*Chris* . . . . Kevork Malikyan
Dave . . . . .Glynn Edwards	*Nick* . . . . .Marc Zuber
Maurice . . . . Anthony Valentine	*Stella* . . . . .Marina Sirtis
Casino manager . . . . David Baron	
Ari . . . . Antony Scott	
Zardinidis . . . . .Dimitri Andreas	Producers . . Lloyd Shirley, George Taylor
Doxiadis . . . . .Harry Tardios	Director . . . . Roy Ward Baker
Andy . . . . .Andy Pantelidou	Executive Producer . . . Verity Lambert

Arthur's friend Maurice, a professional gambler, is barred from the casinos because he is too successful, and is mugged and loses his winnings on the way home. There is an illegal club in Camden Town run by some Greeks where he wants to try to recoup his losses but he needs Terry to accompany him as his bodyguard.

After losing £6,000 on roulette at the club, Maurice suspects that the game is crooked but needs one last chance to prove it. But he has no money left. He sells Arthur his Lotus sports car on the understanding that he can buy it back the following day with his winnings. Maurice comes out winning but finds himself in hospital after a car chase.

Episode 7

Season 1/7   First transmission: 10 December 1979

The Bengal Tiger
by Leon Griffiths

Terry . . . . Dennis Waterman	*Elderly man* . . . . .Roy Evans
Arthur . . . . .George Cole	*Kev* . . . . Mike Grady
Car owner . . . . Graham Stark	*Immigration officer* . . . . Michael Fleming
Mukerjee . . . . .Saeed Jaffrey	*Keith* . . . . Spencer Banks
Norman Gibbons . . . . .Clive Hornby	*Drunken youth* . . . . .Tony London
Barman . . . . .Eamonn Boyce	*Young diner* . . . . . . .Christopher Scoular
Harry . . . . .Edwin Brown	
Indira . . . . Shireen Anwar	Producers . . .Lloyd Shirley, George Taylor
Aslam . . . . Ahmed Khalil	Director . . . . .Peter Sasdy
Wilson . . . . .Stanley Lebor	Executive Producer . . .Verity Lambert

Terry has doubts about his line of work when he has to repossess a car from a customer (played by Graham Stark) who is unable to pay because his firm is out on strike. Arthur, meanwhile, has found Terry a job minding a newsagent's shop after the owner, Mr Mukerjee, has had bricks thrown through his window and has received demands for protection money. But Terry discovers that it is not so simple. Mr Mukerjee has promised his daughter Indira to several prospective Indian husbands and has received bride money in return. The families now want their money returned. Indira is not interested in an arranged marriage to a man she doesn't know and wants to marry her English boyfriend instead. When Indira goes missing, Terry and Arthur act as intermediaries in the negotiations for her return.

Episode 8

First transmission: 17 December 1979

Come in T-64, Your Time is Ticking Away
by Tony Hoare

Terry	. . . . .Dennis Waterman		*Greg*	. . . . .Charlie Hawkins
Arthur	. . . . George Cole		*Katie*	. . . . .Daphne Anderson
Minicab driver	. . . . Michael Hughes		*John*	. . . . .Morgan Sheppard
Woman in flat	. . . . Vicki Woolf		*Dave*	. . . . .Oscar James
Paddy	. . . . .Eric Mason		*Debbie*	. . . . Diana Malin
Kevin	. . . . Alfred Burke			
Des	. . . . George Layton		Producers	. . Lloyd Shirley, George Taylor
Barry	. . . . .Michael Bruce		Director	. . . . .Francis Megahy
Billy	. . . . Darryl Read		Executive Producer	. . . Verity Lambert

When the minicab firm of which Arthur is a co-partner experiences assaults on its drivers and vandalism of its cars, Kevin, the other partner, is reluctant to call in the police because he wants to avoid attracting the interest of the tax authorities. Instead, Arthur recruits Terry as a driver to locate the source of the trouble from the inside. Kevin, in the meantime, becomes interested in buying out Arthur's share of the business. Terry manages to track down the troublemakers, and discovers who is behind the attacks and why Kevin wants to buy Arthur out.

This is the first of five appearances in the programme of Diana Malin as Terry's girlfriend Debbie, a stripper at a local club.

Subplots: Terry acts as a sparring partner at the gym. He buys an old banger from Des to use as his minicab and makes a profit when the car is resold. Arthur is left minding the telephones and has trouble coping.

Episode 9

First transmission: 7 January 1980

Monday Night Fever
by Leon Griffiths

Terry . . . . Dennis Waterman	*Sharon* . . . . Sheila White
Arthur . . . . George Cole	*Freddie* . . . . Michael Melia
Dave . . . . Glynn Edwards	*Penny* . . . . Gennie Nevinson
Disco group . . . . Flint	*Vic Piner* . . . . Anthony Heaton
Barry . . . . Peter Blake	*Henry Piner* . . . . Tommy Wright
Sammy . . . . Aaron Shirley	
Big John . . . . Brian Croucher	
Chris Lambert . . . . Eric Deacon	Producers . . .Lloyd Shirley, George Taylor
Alan . . . . Richard Hunter	Director . . . . Mike Vardy
Chisholm . . . . Patrick Malahide	Executive Producer . . .Verity Lambert

While Terry is standing in as a bouncer at a music club, Arthur becomes infatuated with Sharon Nightingale, an attractive girl who wants to become a singer but has little talent. But Arthur promises to make her a star. In the process, he finds himself badly out of pocket and in trouble with 'er indoors. To add to his problems, he finds that his lockup has been broken into and that Chisholm is taking an unhealthy interest in its contents. This episode sees the first of four appearances of Gennie Nevinson as Terry's girlfriend Penny, an air stewardess.

Episode 10

First transmission: 14 January 1980

The Dessert Song
by Andrew Payne

Terry	Dennis Waterman		*Omar*	Godfrey James
Arthur	George Cole		*Hilditch*	Ian Barritt
Dave	Glynn Edwards		*Harry*	David Sinclair
Mario	Bruno Barnabe		*Drunk in pub*	Jonathan Hackett
Charlie	Peter Bland			
Nick	Michael Angelis		Producers	Lloyd Shirley, George Taylor
Christina	Diane Keen		Director	Roy Ward Baker
Johnny	Daniel Hill		Executive Producer	Verity Lambert

While trying to shift a job lot of tinned pickled walnuts, Arthur and Terry come across Charlie, a newly arrived Greek Cypriot, being attacked by three thugs. Charlie asks for a lift to the restaurant where he is staying with his widowed cousin Christina. She later traces Arthur to the Winchester Club and asks for his help in protecting her against her late husband's brother Omar who is trying to force her to give up her husband's share of the restaurant. Arthur assigns Terry to mind the restaurant. Charlie then appears at the Winchester Club seeking transport to collect some left luggage from the railway station. They discover that the luggage contains a sawn-off shotgun that Charlie is planning to use on the man who murdered his brother in Cyprus.

Episode 11

First transmission: 21 January 1980

You Gotta Have Friends
by Leon Griffiths

Terry	Dennis Waterman	*Alan*	Brian Hall
Arthur	George Cole	*Stuart*	Prentis Hancock
Billy Gilpin	David Buck	*Altman*	George Baker
Valerie	Denise Distel	*Lady Ingrave*	Deborah Grant
First detective	Terence Budd		
DI Barnett	Allan Surtees	Producers	Lloyd Shirley, George Taylor
Whaley	Roy Kinnear	Director	Ian Toynton
George	Gary Whelan	Executive Producer	Verity Lambert

Returning home from a 'function' (presumably Masonic but this is not specified), Arthur finds his old friend Billy Gilpin waiting for him, bruised and beaten up and needing a lift to the coast. Arthur is too drunk to drive and asks Terry to take Billy where he wants to go. When Terry returns, he finds two police officers waiting to question him about Billy's whereabouts because Billy is wanted for attempted murder.

Lady Ingrave, whose husband was the intended murder victim, has a lucrative racket selling fake bearer bonds in Europe. When £70,000 goes missing, her partner suspects that Arthur is involved and sends his heavies to recover the money. Terry discovers where the money is and manages to return it — just in time to prevent serious damage to Arthur's health. There is a good visual effect when a car overturns on Hampstead Heath.

Episode 12

Season 2/1   First transmission: 11 September 1980

National Pelmet

by Willis Hall

Terry . . . . Dennis Waterman	*Jeremy Burnham-Jones* . . . . Robert Swann
Arthur . . . . George Cole	*Clerk of the scales* . . . . . . Raymond Young
Jocelyn . . . . Liza Goddard	*Georgie Gumm* . . . . Billy Kerry
Everett . . . . Jeremy Young	
Bookie . . . . John Fahey	
O'Brady . . . . Jim Norton	Producers . . Lloyd Shirley, George Taylor
Rita . . . . Jane Carr	Director . . . . Martin Campbell
Brickett . . . . Ken Hutchison	Executive Producer . . . Verity Lambert

Arthur approaches an antique dealer, the Hon. Jeremy Burnham-Jones, to help shift some china figurines of the poet Milton. Jones, in return, asks Terry to mind Pelmet, his racehorse, which he suspects may be the target of a doping attempt before a big race. Initially unwilling to spend his nights with a horse, Terry is eventually persuaded when he meets Jocelyn, the jockey. However, it is the stable girl Rita who Terry discovers is particularly attracted to him.

The night before the race, an intruder sets fire to the stable but escapes while Terry is leading the horse to safety. Terry recognises the intruder the next day at the race meeting and manages to apprehend him with Rita's help. He then discovers the reason for the arson attack. The fire at the stable provides a spectacular visual effect.

The *TV Times* (6/9/80) reported that this episode was originally set in the world of greyhound racing but the National Greyhound Racing Association did not approve of the story line. In the absence of a suitable location for the greyhound story, the episode was rewritten around horse racing.

Episode 13

Season 2/2   First transmission: 18 September 1980

Whose Wife is it Anyway
by Tony Hoare

Terry	Dennis Waterman	*Ronald*	Brian Jameson
Arthur	George Cole	*Garry*	Stuart St Paul
Dave	Glynn Edwards	*George*	John Forgeham
Nursing sister	Victoria Fenton	*Charlie*	Peter Cheevers
Alex	David Daker	*Policeman*	Charles Pemberton
Terry's gran	Molly Veness		
Jim	Alun Lewis	Producers	Lloyd Shirley, George Taylor
Chas	David Auker	Director	Roy Ward Baker
Gloria	Janet Key	Executive Producer	Verity Lambert

Alex, previously a villain but now legitimate and running an antique shop, has been injured in a hit-and-run accident. Alex's partner Jim has reported that two heavies were in the shop recently demanding protection money. Arthur arranges for Terry to spend some time in the shop in case they return. Terry's enthusiasm for the job is dampened when he finds that Jim is gay. He also gets an uncomfortable feeling about the case when he discovers that none of the other antique shops on the manor have had demands. His suspicions are heightened after he meets Alex's ex-wife Gloria. Arthur and Terry discover that first impressions can be misleading.

Subplot: Arthur is selling dodgy wristwatches.

Episode 14

Season 2/3   First transmission: 25 September 1980

You Lose Some, You Win Some
by Jeremy Burnham

Terry	Dennis Waterman	*Maureen*	Lesley Joseph
Arthur	George Cole	*Sadie*	Lynda Baron
Penny	Gennie Nevinson	*Mrs Beecham*	Peggy Thorpe-Bates
Jackie	Beth Morris	*Miss Carr*	Angela Easterling
Jackson	Kenneth Midwood	*Women at health farm*	Toni Palmer,
Maurice	Anthony Valentine		Pamela Manson
Alnutt	Clifford Parrish		
Tony	Michael Watkins		
George	Sidney Livingstone	Producers	Lloyd Shirley, George Taylor
Parsons	Leslie Schofield	Director	James Gatward
Major Lampson	Ronald Leigh-Hunt	Executive Producer	Verity Lambert

Maurice, the professional gambler who appeared in Episode 6, has promised his wife he will give up gambling but is now running a roulette syndicate at the casino. The syndicate members use their own money and Maurice collects 50 percent of the profits. When one of the members has a big win, Maurice has some trouble with a bouncer and is removed from the club. The syndicate must keep all its members in order to be successful but Maurice is concerned that the club will intimidate the syndicate members and force them to leave. He asks Arthur for Terry's help to protect them.

Terry is unenthusiastic as he had planned to spend the week with Penny, his air-hostess girlfriend, but the offer of £600 for a week's work is too good to pass up. When Terry overhears a bouncer threatening one of the syndicate, Arthur moves them all to Terry's place for protection. But then Maurice's wife goes missing and Terry, Arthur, and Maurice set out to find her.

Episode 15

Season 2/4   First transmission: 9 October 1980

Don't Tell Them Willie Boy Was Here
by Paul Wheeler

Terry . . . . Dennis Waterman	*Trudy* . . . . Mandy Perryment
Arthur . . . . George Cole	*Girl in disco* . . . . Imogen Bickford-Smith
Dave . . . . Glynn Edwards	*Ruth Reynolds* . . . . Tania Rogers
TV compere . . . . Ronnie Stevens	*Fashion photographer* . . . . Barry Wade
Herself . . . . Jackie Collins	*Jack Straw* . . . . Alex Tompkins
Willie Reynolds . . . . Paul Barber	*Boxing commentator* . . . . Benny Lee
Barney Mather . . . . Alfred Marks	
Sparring partner . . . . Eddie Stacey	Producers . . . Lloyd Shirley, George Taylor
Pug . . . . Dinny Powell	Director . . . . Dennis Abey
Sarah Jane . . . . Vicki Michelle	Executive Producer . . . Verity Lambert

Willie Reynolds, who was once a champion boxer, returns to England for a comeback fight after a two-year absence. Barney Mather, the promoter, is worried about Willie's attitude towards the fight and asks Arthur if Terry can keep an eye on Willie. Alone with Terry, Willie confides that he has lost the will to fight but needs the £20,000 loser's purse to pay off his tax bill. When Arthur hears about Willie's weakness he tries to manipulate the odds to profit from Willie's defeat. However, when Willie hears that the odds are rigged against him he starts to take the fight seriously. Look out for a guest appearance of Jackie Collins playing herself on the fictitious Joel Bray TV talk show.

Episode 16

First transmission: 16 October 1980

Not a Bad Lad, Dad
by Tony Hoare

Terry	Dennis Waterman	*Ronnie*	Dicken Ashworth
Arthur	George Cole	*Disco youths*	Ray Burdis,
Dave	Glynn Edwards		Nicholas Diprose
Peter	Warren O'Neill	*Duty sergeant*	Geoffrey Leesley
Beryl	Sharon Duce		
Mary	Lesley Clare O'Niell		
Bob	Martin Bax	Producers	Lloyd Shirley, George Taylor
Publican	Stanley Price	Director	Ian Toynton
Penny	Gennie Nevinson	Executive Producer	Verity Lambert

In this unusually sensitive episode, Terry finds nine-year-old Peter sitting on his doorstep with a letter from his mother claiming that Peter is Terry's son. Terry finds himself looking after the boy and playing the role of a father. The episode highlights the problem of marital violence but is let down by a schmaltzy ending.

Subplots: Arthur is selling dodgy booze and Terry is minding a disco.

Episode 17

Season 2/6   First transmission: 23 October 1980

The Beer Hunter
by Willis Hall

Terry . . . . Dennis Waterman	*Renee* . . . . Georgina Hale
Arthur . . . . George Cole	*Chef* . . . . Alan David
Police constable . . . . William Rourke	*Dora* . . . . Pat Ashton
Yorkie . . . . Brian Glover	*Reg* . . . . Barrie Rutter
Enrico . . . . Victor Baring	*Brenda* . . . . Jo Warne
Coliver . . . . Robert Blythe	
Carol . . . . Janine Duvitski	Producers . . .Lloyd Shirley, George Taylor
Carlos . . . . Carlos Douglas	Director . . . . Tom Clegg
Trev . . . . Marshall Ward	Executive Producer . . .Verity Lambert

Arthur's old army pal Yorkie goes missing from his hotel the morning after their army reunion dinner. Yorkie's wife is due to arrive at Victoria Coach Station that afternoon and Arthur is terrified of the consequences of not being able to produce Yorkie.

Yorkie wakes up in bed with Renee, who claims to be a part-time model. She explains to Yorkie that he was delivered to her place by a one-armed minicab driver and was so drunk when he arrived that he threw his trousers out of the window. Unable to remember the name of his hotel, he and Renee begin a laborious search through the telephone directory looking for a familiar name. Terry, meanwhile, goes back to the hotel where he originally dropped Yorkie but the hotel denies all knowledge of him. Terry and Arthur trace the minicab driver and manage to track Yorkie down. But the bus from up north has already arrived at the coach station. . . .

Subplots: Arthur demonstrates his prowess on the rugby field, and nearly causes a punch-up between a bride and groom as they leave the church.

Episode 18

Season 2/7   First transmission: 30 October 1980

A Nice Little Wine
by Stanley Price

Terry	Dennis Waterman	*Sandra*	Lois Baxter
Arthur	George Cole	*Sandra's mum*	Pam St Clement
Dave	Glynn Edwards	*Policeman*	Davyd Harries
Clive	Peter Jeffrey	*Sojo*	Burt Kwouk
Joan	Diana Berriman	*Chisholm*	Patrick Malahide
George	Ron Pember		
Bettina	Rachel Davies		
1st winetaster	Michael Logan	*Producers*	Lloyd Shirley, George Taylor
2nd winetaster	James Griffiths	*Director*	Chris Menaul
Scots winetaster	Donald Douglas	*Executive Producer*	Verity Lambert

After selling Arthur a bargain consignment of red wine, Clive is drugged and robbed by a masseuse in his hotel room. Arthur gets blamed for setting up the robbery and is given three days to return the stolen money or else he will be turned over to some undesirable people. Terry checks into the hotel to investigate and tracks down the culprit to a dodgy escort agency run from a sex shop. However, before he can return the stolen money, Arthur discovers that Sergeant Chisholm also has an interest in Clive.

Look out for a small part for Pam St Clement, who later became better known as Pat in *EastEnders*.

Episode 19

Season 2/8   First transmission: 6 November 1980

All Mod Cons
by Andrew Payne

Terry . . . . Dennis Waterman	*Filmer* . . . . Michael O'Hagan
Arthur . . . . .George Cole	*Kate* . . . . Toyah Willcox
Dave . . . . Glynn Edwards	*Vickery* . . . . James Ottaway
Harry . . . . .Harry Towb	*Pearce* . . . . Tony Osoba
Bellars . . . . Douglas Reith	*Rita* .Sara Clee
Boardman . . . . Michael Jayes	*Shirley* . . . . .Frances Low
Simon . . . . .Simon Cadell	
Helen . . . . Annette Lynton	Producers . . .Lloyd Shirley, George Taylor
Bernie . . . . .Mike Savage	Director . . . . Ian Sharp
Jack McQueen . . . . .Michael Robbins	Executive Producer . . .Verity Lambert

Charlie Vickery asks Arthur to help him remove some squatters from a dilapidated house that he wants to subdivide into flats. When Terry goes to confront the squatters he discovers a young couple with a baby who claim that they are paying rent for the property. Terry subsequently discovers that the rent collector is Vickery's granddaughter Kate. When Kate realises that Terry has not removed the couple she hires some thugs to force them out. Look out for Toyah Willcox playing the unscrupulous Kate, and another appearance of Terry's Ford Capri, SLE 71R.

Subplots: Terry takes a job as a bouncer at the club where Helen, his new girlfriend, works and discovers that the manager is fiddling the books. Without Terry's knowledge, Arthur plans to re-let Terry's flat to Jack McQueen who wants it for Shirley, who he claims is his niece. Arthur stores a consignment of toilet bowls in the yard of the Winchester Club — and buys a bidet for 'er indoors.

Episode 20

Season 2/9   First transmission: 20 November 1980

Diamonds are a Girl's Worst Enemy
by Paul Wheeler

Terry	Dennis Waterman	*Sid*	Sam Kydd
Arthur	George Cole	*First player*	Charles Cork
Dave	Glynn Edwards	*Second player*	John Mulcahy
Rose	Ann Lynn	*Jack*	Tony Selby
Driver	Howard Attfield	*Yoyo Pickles*	Leo Dolan
Miss Cawley	Celia Foxe		
Tajvir	Zia Mohyeddin	Producers	Lloyd Shirley, George Taylor
Des	George Layton	Director	Chris King
Harrison	John Ringham	Executive Producer	Verity Lambert

Terry's cushy little job driving a Mercedes 450SEL for Rose Mellor (whose husband is inside doing a 15-stretch) loses its attraction when the car is stolen along with £100,000-worth of uncut diamonds hidden inside the car. Mr Tefkin, the owner of the diamonds, is livid and threatens Arthur and Terry with physical harm if the diamonds are not recovered within 24 hours. Terry seeks help from his pal Des but is not able to track down the car through the underworld car trade. Concerned for his safety, Arthur seeks help from the police in finding the car. But Rose is more interested in a foam bath and champagne with Terry than in finding her missing car.

When the car is found smashed into a lamppost opposite Surbiton police station, minus the diamonds, Terry realises that he and Arthur have been set up.

This episode is a loose follow-on to Episode 2 in the first season.

Episode 21

First transmission: 27 November 1980

The Old School Tie
by Jeremy Burnham

Terry . . . . Dennis Waterman	*Kevin Wells* . . . . Paul Moriarty
Arthur . . . . .George Cole	*Tommy* . . . . Nick Stringer
Dave . . . . Glynn Edwards	*Billy* . . . . Ziggy Byfield
Palmer . . . . Paul Copley	*Jacobson* . . . . Harold Berens
Debbie . . . . Diana Malin	
Rycott . . . . .Peter Childs	Producers . . .Lloyd Shirley, George Taylor
Olive . . . . .Sherrie Hewson	Director . . . . James Gatward
Harry . . . . Derek Thompson	Executive Producer . . .Verity Lambert

This episode, dealing with school-day loyalties, is full of violence and contains a convincing fight sequence in a car-breaker's yard.

Terry's old schoolmate George Palmer escapes from prison with only three months of his sentence left to serve. He breaks into Terry's flat and asks Terry to help him prove his innocence. He claims that he was doing a housebreaking job a couple of streets away and just happened to be in the vicinity of the diamond robbery for which he was sentenced. Terry arranges with Dave for him to stay in the attic of the Winchester Club but soon discovers that it is not only the police who are looking for Palmer. Two heavies beat up Terry's girlfriend Debbie, smash Arthur's lockup, and give Dave a beating in order to find Palmer. With the help of Palmer's wife, her brother, and a reporter, Terry gets a good idea where Palmer is being held and who was responsible for the diamond robbery. He rescues Palmer — but not without a fight.

Subplots: Arthur is selling dodgy golf clubs, and he and Terry part company over a favour Terry does for a friend.

Episode 22

Season 2/11   First transmission: 4 December 1980

All About Scoring, Innit
by Willis Hall

Terry	Dennis Waterman	*Leo Rafferty*	Sean Caffrey
Arthur	George Cole	*Clifton Fields*	George Sweeney
Dave	Glynn Edwards	*Jenny*	Adrienne Posta
Danny Varrow	Karl Howman	*Barmaid*	Mitzi Rogers
Arklow	Forbes Collins	*Reporter*	Martin Neil
Ronnie Raikes	Anthony Douse	*Student nurse*	Nikola Rowley
Mini-cab driver	Dino Shafeek		
Club receptionist	Rachel Herbert	Producers	Lloyd Shirley, George Taylor
Police sergeant	Bill Dean	Director	Martin Campbell
Robbie Costello	Malcolm Hayes	Executive Producer	Verity Lambert

Danny Varrow is a famous footballer with a reputation for gambling, drinking and womanising. When he goes missing and wants to sell his story to the newspapers, Arthur sees the chance of a quick commission. Arthur assigns Terry to mind Varrow at Terry's flat while Arthur tries to locate sports-writer Ronnie Raikes and do a deal on the story. Varrow has grander ideas and insists that they check into a hotel penthouse suite. Unknown to any of them, there are other people anxious to find Varrow. By the time Arthur tracks down Ronnie Raikes, Varrow has been abducted from the hotel. Terry has to act quickly to prevent Varrow from getting hurt and sustains a shotgun wound in the process.

This episode contains actual footage of a 1980 football match between Chelsea and Preston.

Episode 23

First transmission: 11 December 1980

Caught in the Act, Fact
by Tony Hoare

Terry	Dennis Waterman	*Mr Knight*	Angus Mackay
Arthur	George Cole	*Lady Margaret Thompson*	Angela Browne
Dave	Glynn Edwards	*Housewife*	Veronica Clifford
Harry	Glyn Houston	*Collin*	John Rolfe
Des	George Layton	*Magistrate*	Ellis Dale
Bertie	James Marcus		
Stevie	Colin Prockter	Producers	Lloyd Shirley, George Taylor
Chisholm	Patrick Malahide	Director	Terry Green
DC Jones	Ken Sharrock	Executive Producer	Verity Lambert

Terry's fingerprints are found on a car used in a robbery and Chisholm takes him in as a suspect. Arthur, meanwhile, has found Terry a job driving for Lady Margaret Thompson. Arthur neglects to warn Terry about Lady Margaret's shoplifting problem and Terry finds himself accused of shop theft when he goes shopping with Lady Margaret and leaves the store carrying one of her bags containing unpaid items. When the Thompsons deny all knowledge of Arthur and Terry, Chisholm persuades Terry to plead guilty in return for a favourable police report.

Subplot: Arthur employs Stevie to drive around the housing estates offering goldfish in plastic bags to children in exchange for used clothes which he intends to resell.

Sergeant Chisholm's detective constable in this episode, played by Ken Sharrock, is listed in the credits as DC Jones. This character was actually played by Welsh actor Michael Povey for 21 episodes as from the beginning of the next season.

This episode was originally intended to be the last in the season, and there is a cliffhanger ending in which Arthur and Terry part company and go their separate ways. Instead, the episode was followed the next week by *A Lot of Bull and a Pat on the Back*, which was pre-empted from its originally scheduled transmission on 2 October 1980.

Episode 24

First transmission: 18 December 1980

A Lot of Bull and a Pat on the Back
by Tony Hoare

Terry	Dennis Waterman	*Shop assistant*	Max Mason
Arthur	George Cole	*Bella*	Ann Bruce
Dave	Glynn Edwards	*Heavy*	Richard Cubison
Debbie	Diana Malin	*Policeman*	Leonard Braden
Penny	Gennie Nevinson		
Smith	Leon Sinden	Producers	Lloyd Shirley, George Taylor
Brown	Derek Benfield	Director	Terry Green
Creasey	Ken Wynne	Executive Producer	Verity Lambert

Terry is looking forward to three days' holiday with his girlfriend Penny. Arthur upsets these plans when he is approached by two farmers who ask for his help in repossessing a prize bull in return for a generous fee. But after repossessing the bull and delivering it as requested, Arthur and Terry discover from the newspaper that they have actually stolen the bull. The only solution is to repossess it once again and return it to its rightful owner. Look out for an unscripted scene in which Arthur slips over in the field and lands in a cowpat. The director liked the scene so much that he left it in the final footage.

Subplot: Terry's stripper friend Debbie has been threatened at the strip club by a man who wants to get her into prostitution. The club owner does not want to involve the police so Debbie asks for Terry's help.

Episode 25

         First transmission: 13 January 1982

Dead Men Do Tell Tales
by Tony Hoare

Terry	Dennis Waterman	*Mrs Chambers' mother*	Eileen Way
Arthur	George Cole	*Chisholm*	Patrick Malahide
Dave	Glynn Edwards	*DC Jones*	Micheal Povey
Mrs Chambers	Patricia Maynard	*Vicar*	Michael Jenkinson
Monty Wiseman	Harry Fowler		
Randolf	Rayner Bourton		
Nancy	Suzy Quatro	Producers	Lloyd Shirley, George Taylor
Meadhurst	Derek Fowlds	Director	Robert Young
Incapable	Harold Innocent	Executive Producer	Verity Lambert

Joe Chambers has died overseas and Arthur's business associate Monty Wiseman is helping Mrs Chambers repatriate the body. In a highly implausible scenario, Monty arranges with Arthur to store the coffin and the body in his lockup until the funeral because Meadhurst the undertaker has no room to accommodate it on his premises. Meadhurst subsequently discovers that the coroner has ordered an inquest and that he has to collect the body from the lockup and deliver it to the mortuary for an autopsy. On hearing this news, Wiseman forces Arthur to move the coffin out of the lockup before it can be collected by the undertaker. Arthur arranges for it to go to Terry's flat, knowing that Terry is currently out with his new girlfriend Nancy, a grass-smoking rock singer (played by rock singer Suzy Quatro). Wiseman then becomes very anxious to contact an alcoholic tramp known as 'Incapable'. Chisholm later discovers why Wiseman was so keen to contact Incapable before the autopsy.

When the episode was first shown, it was preceded by a warning about the sensitive nature of the story line.

Episode 26

Season 3/2   First transmission: 20 January 1982

You Need Hands
by Andrew Payne

Terry	Dennis Waterman	*Old man*	Leslie Sarony
Arthur	George Cole	*Bowman's heavy*	Terry Gurry
Dave	Glynn Edwards	*Lenny Bowman*	Harry Landis
Des	George Layton	*Vernon*	Mike Reid
Security guard	Martin Fisk	*Merrick*	Alan MacNaughtan
Gerry	Gareth Milne	*Merrick's heavy*	Steve Emerson
Mick	Richard Clay-Jones		
Matthews	Julian Holloway	Producers	Lloyd Shirley, George Taylor
Julie	Debby Cumming	Director	Ian Sharp
Carol	Nicola Kimber	Executive Producer	Verity Lambert

Arthur offers Terry as a bodyguard to accompany Matthews, a diamond dealer, while he is delivering a package of diamonds to a dealer in the City. But unknown to Arthur, Terry has broken his arm in a scuffle. Matthews is not prepared to use an injured bodyguard and Arthur recruits Vernon, a minder with a taste for gourmet food and wine, to replace Terry. Unable to work for Arthur, Terry helps Des chase up some money he is owed and they stumble upon a distribution network for illicit drugs.

Meanwhile, Matthews delivers the package safely under Vernon's protection. Unaware that the contents were actually heroin and not diamonds, Arthur is told that the first consignment was a rehearsal and that the real transaction will take place the following morning in a deserted field. Unwilling to allow Arthur to be left alone, Matthews insists that he, Arthur and Vernon remain in the car together overnight.

Sensitivities about illegal drugs led to a warning to viewers before this episode was first shown.

Episode 27

Season 3/3   First transmission: 27 January 1982

Rembrandt Doesn't Live Here Anymore
by Dave Humphries

Terry	Dennis Waterman	*Peter*	Paul Gregory
Arthur	George Cole	*Gerry*	Val Musetti
Dave	Glynn Edwards	*Quinn's assistant*	Douglas McFerran
Stripper	Candy Davis	*Kevin*	Steve Alder
Male dancer	Roy Pannell	*First heavy*	Peter Brayham
Frank	George Sewell	*Second heavy*	Dave Holland
Max	John Tordoff		
Rory Quinn	Ewan Hooper	Producers	Lloyd Shirley, George Taylor
Second stripper	Monica Ramone	Director	Tom Clegg
Monica	Patricia Quinn	Executive Producer	Verity Lambert

While visiting a strip club where Terry is working as a temporary bouncer, Arthur meets up with an old pal, Frankie Simmons, a talented forger. Frankie now makes a living making high quality copies of old paintings that can be sold at auction for several thousand pounds. Arthur sees that there may be some entrepreneurial opportunities in the business and arranges for Terry to collect one of Frankie's paintings to sell to Peter, an art dealer. Unknown to Arthur, Peter recognises the painting as a fake but realises that he could sell similar paintings overseas for a substantial profit. Encouraged by his initial success, Arthur sells another painting, this time to Rory Quinn. Rory is initially pleased with his purchase — until he notices something that proves it is not an original.

Subplot: Frankie's flatmate Monica seeks Terry's help in persuading Frankie to move out because her boyfriend is expected back any day.

Episode 28

Season 3/4   First transmission: 3 February 1982

Looking for Micky
by Tony Hoare

Terry . . . . .Dennis Waterman	*Freddie Baker* . . . . .John Moffatt
Arthur . . . . George Cole	*Alan* . . . . Terry Plummer
Dave . . . . Glynn Edwards	*Billy* . . . . Stephen Phillips
Micky . . . . John Labanowski	*Housewife* . . . . Marcia Tucker
George . . . . .Jim McManus	*John Oates* . . . . Bill Nighy
Debbie . . . . Diana Malin	*Editor* . . . . Richard Simpson
Anker . . . . Tom Watson	
Chisholm . . . . Patrick Malahide	Producers . . Lloyd Shirley, George Taylor
DC Jones . . . . .Michael Povey	Director . . . . Tom Clegg
Queenie . . . . Vanda Godsell	Executive Producer . . . Verity Lambert

'Mad' Micky, who knows Terry from their boxing days, is serving an indefinite
prison sentence for crimes of violence. He escapes from prison and finds his
way to the home of Terry's stripper friend Debbie who is also an old friend.
Micky wants Terry to help him make a protest about the unfairness of his
sentence and to try to obtain a definite release date. When Arthur hears about
it he sees the chance of a journalistic scoop and tries to interest a Fleet Street
reporter, John Oates, in Micky's story by making a video of Micky. Micky's
previous boxing manager, Freddie Baker, also has an interest in finding Micky
and traces him to Debbie's place. Oates gets a story, but not the one that
Arthur expected.

Subplot: Arthur is selling dog's tooth sports jackets.

Episode 29

Season 3/5   First transmission: 10 February 1982

Dreamhouse
by Andrew Payne

Terry	Dennis Waterman	*Shades 2*	Niall Padden
Arthur	George Cole	*Barbara*	Sandy Ratcliff
Dave	Glynn Edwards	*Janet*	Emma Williams
Beryl	Wanda Ventham	*Bernard*	Clive Mantle
Kenny	Dave Atkins	*Stanley*	Adrian Mills
Receptionist	Sylvia O'Donnell		
Silver	Roger Sloman		
Derek Farrow	Richard Griffiths	Producers	Lloyd Shirley, George Taylor
Woods	Frank Coda	Director	Tom Clegg
Shades 1	Ken Kitson	Executive Producer	Verity Lambert

Frankie Farrow was a famous pop singer in the 1960s. His manager, Georgie Silver, arranges with Arthur for Terry to mind Frankie's mansion, known as the Dreamhouse, while Frankie is performing in Las Vegas. At the Dreamhouse, Terry discovers Frankie's brother Derek who was once Frankie's accountant and personal assistant but was subsequently fired after a sordid court case and is now a jobless alcoholic. Arthur, meanwhile, is doing a deal on the purchase of three coin-operated children's rides and borrows the money from the recently widowed Beryl. Arthur falls victim to a con trick and has to break the news to Beryl that he has lost the money, but discovers that she has things other than money on her mind. When two heavies appear at the Dreamhouse, Terry discovers that Frankie is not performing in Las Vegas at all but is living in Spain after working on his own money-making scheme up North. But by then the Dreamhouse has become a focus for several people with scores to settle.

Episode 30
Season 3/6   First transmission: 17 February 1982

Another Bride, Another Groom
by Willis Hall

Terry . . . . .Dennis Waterman	*Middle-aged man* . . . . .Jeffrey Segal
Arthur . . . . George Cole	*Malcolm* . . . . Roger Kemp
Dave . . . . .Glynn Edwards	*Trina* . . . . .Jayne Lester
Stan . . . . Richard Williams	*Groomsman* . . . . .Michael Garner
Noisy . . . . John Judd	*Photographer* . . . . Ivor Danvers
Bernie . . . . .John Hartley	*Grantley* . . . . .Ian Hogg
Readies . . . . .Peter Holt	
Darrell . . . . .Mark Botham	
Reggie . . . . Desmond McNamara	
DC Ashmole . . . . Warren Clarke	Producers . . Lloyd Shirley, George Taylor
Middle-aged ladies . . . . Maggie Flint,	Director . . . . Mike Vardy
. . . . .Barbara Ashcroft	Executive Producer . . . Verity Lambert

In the midst of organising his niece's wedding day, Arthur finds himself having to take delivery of a load of pornographic magazines. Terry is assigned to collect them in the bridal car from a sex shop in Watford and deliver the bride and her father to the church on the way back. He is trailed by Ashmole, a corrupt police officer, in one car, and by three heavies in another. When Terry arrives at the church, the heavies force him to visit Mr Grantley, the rightful owner of the magazines. Arthur too is dragged off to visit Grantley — who intends to set an example for the theft of his goods. Arthur and Terry return to the wedding reception in time for Terry to take the happy couple to the airport for their honeymoon. But even this does not work out smoothly.

Episode 31

Season 3/7 First transmission: 24 February 1982

The Birdman of Wormwood Scrubs
by Leon Griffiths

Terry	Dennis Waterman	Bank manager	Frederick Treves
Arthur	George Cole	Mrs Knight	Avril Angers
Spencer	Stephen Grief		
Kate	Rula Lenska		
Billings	Maurice Denham		
Ernie	Max Wall	Producers	Lloyd Shirley, George Taylor
Shop assistant	Charles Rogers	Director	Ian Toynton
Grundy	Joe Ritchie	Executive Producer	Verity Lambert

Arthur and Terry meet Ernie Dodds on his release from a 14-year prison sentence. Unwillingly subsidised by Arthur, Ernie goes on a spending spree and books into an expensive hotel while he waits to withdraw the proceeds of the robbery from a secret bank account. He discovers, however, that the account was closed several years ago while he was in prison. He suspects the bank manager, who is now dead, of having defrauded him. They soon discover that several other parties are interested in getting a share of the proceeds. Terry and Ernie visit the bank manager's widow and discover that her late husband lost all his money in bad business deals. All she has left is a pet shop. An arrangement is agreed upon which can make use of the knowledge of natural history that Ernie acquired in prison.

Episode 32

Season 3/8

First transmission: 3 March 1982

The Son Also Rises
by Paul Wheeler

Terry . . . . .Dennis Waterman	*John Standen* . . . . Stephen Garlick
Arthur . . . . George Cole	*Schoolboy* . . . . Kevin Hart
Dave . . . . .Glynn Edwards	*First youth* . . . . Ozzie Stevens
Alex Rowan . . . . .Gary Waldhorn	*Second youth* . . . . Steve Fletcher
Phil . . . . David Arlen	*Morrie Levin* . . . . .Alfie Bass
Morley . . . . Christopher Coll	*Ronald* . . . . .Nigel Humphreys
Muriel Standen . . . . . Annabel Leventon	
Ted Standen . . . . .Gareth Hunt	Producers . . Lloyd Shirley, George Taylor
Julie . . . . Bobbie Brown	Director . . . . .Francis Megahy
Standen's heavy . . . . . Christopher Ellison	Executive Producer . . . Verity Lambert

Alex Rowan, once a successful accountant, has just been released from prison after serving a sentence for bribery and corruption. His ex-boss Ted Standen, who was also involved in the case but was not charged, is refusing to pay Rowan the £60,000 he was promised to keep Standen's name out of court. Standen is also refusing to pay maintenance to his ex-wife Muriel or school fees for his 17-year-old son John. To put pressure on Standen, Rowan arranges for Standen's son to be roughed up by some young thugs once a week. When Arthur hears about the attacks, he arranges for Terry to mind the boy for a fee. But when Arthur starts receiving threats of violence unless Terry stops minding the boy, he persuades Muriel to close the deal. Meanwhile, two thugs confront Terry and John outside the Winchester Club and Terry establishes that they are working for Rowan. A method is devised to get Standen to pay his dues. Arthur becomes an accountant for the afternoon, Standen's secretary has the last laugh on Standen, and Terry has the last laugh on Arthur.

Episode 33

Season 3/9   First transmission: 10 March 1982

Why Pay Tax
by Leon Griffiths

Terry . . . . Dennis Waterman		*Doctor* . . . . Peter Machin
Arthur . . . . .George Cole		*Mr Wong* . . . . Cecil Cheng
Dave . . . . Glynn Edwards		*Cyril* . . . . Roger Brierley
Dolly . . . . Kika Markham		*Ram* . . . . Ronnie Cush
Settler . . . . .Richard Bartlett		*Woman customer* . . . . . Eliza Buckingham
Forman . . . . .Shay Gorman		
Young policeman . . . . Kevin Barke		
Barry . . . . .Michael Medwin		Producers . . .Lloyd Shirley, George Taylor
Man in car . . . . .Paul Weston		Director . . . . .Roy Ward Baker
Ray . . . . Nigel Davenport		Executive Producer . . .Verity Lambert

Barry, a dubious turf accountant, asks Terry to escort him while he pays out winnings of £16,000 to Ray, one of his punters. Barry accidentally gives the money to the wrong person and Terry is injured trying to recover it. Needing hospital treatment for his injuries, Terry misses his date with Dolly, who was recently widowed from betting shop proprietor Charlie Warner. Terry later discovers that Barry is penniless and that the payment to the wrong person was a set-up to buy time from Ray. Ray, however, does not accept Barry's excuses and removes all the furniture from Barry's flat, threatening to remove one of his arms or legs if the money is not paid up. Learning of Terry's interest in Dolly, Barry borrows the money from her, explaining that it is for Terry who is in trouble. Terry discovers Barry's scheme but finds that Dolly has devised her own way of getting repayment from Barry.

Subplot: Arthur buys a job lot of second-hand fireplaces from a demolition site including one he believes will sell for £5,000.

Episode 34

Season 3/10   First transmission: 17 March 1982

Broken Arrow
by George Day

Terry . . . . .Dennis Waterman	*Little Freddie* . . . . Alfred Maron
Arthur . . . . George Cole	*Woman at Silver Rose* . . . . . Honora Burke
Dave . . . . .Glynn Edwards	*Man at Silver Rose* . . . . Roy Pattison
Dafydd . . . . Sean Mathias	*Eric* . . . . Chris Johnston
Pat . . . . .Paddy Joyce	*Eddie Pitt* . . . . John Joyce
Len . . . . Jonathan Kydd	*Sister* . . . . Virginia Denham
Derek . . . . Gary Olsen	*Caller (Irish pub)* . . . . Mike Kemp
Wally . . . . .Michael Graham Cox	
Sherry . . . . Maggie Steed	Producers . . Lloyd Shirley, George Taylor
Mr Rice . . . . Jestyn Phillips	Director . . . . Roy Ward Baker
Ted . . . . Edward Peel	Executive Producer . . . Verity Lambert

When Arthur discovers that Dafydd, an innocent young Welshman, is an expert darts player, he sponsors a darts tournament to cash in on his talent. Following a successful game in another tournament, however, the organisers injure Dafydd's hand to ensure that he does not play there again. Arthur, meanwhile, is unable to raise the £1,000 prize money and has doubts about Dafydd's ability to play with his left hand.

Subplot: The customised Stingray car that Arthur is trying to sell is vandalised and has to be fixed up by Ted, an Elvis Presley look-alike, who is standing in for Des while he is away on holiday.

Episode 35

Season 3/11   First transmission: 24 March 1982

Poetic Justice, Innit?
by Tony Hoare

Terry . . . . Dennis Waterman	*Mr Russell QC* . . . . . . Bernard Horsfall
Arthur . . . . .George Cole	*Knowles* . . . . Peter-Hugo Daly
Dave . . . . Glynn Edwards	*Roberts* . . . . Stephen Bent
Debbie . . . . Diana Malin	*The jury* . . . . John Bardon,
Waiter . . . . Oscar Narciso	. . . .Anthony Chinn, Anton Darby,
Clerk of the court . . . . Michael Browning	. . . . Lloyd McGuire, David Sibley,
Judge . . . . .James Cossins	.Pamela Cundell, Bridget McConnel,
Smith . . . . .Larry Martyn	. . .Jamila Massey, Gwyneth Strong,
DC Jones . . . . Michael Povey	. . April Walker, Larrington Walker
Chisholm . . . . Patrick Malahide	*Fish shop proprietor* . . . . .Tony Barton
Soames . . . . Michael Culver	
Parsons . . . . Barrie Cookson	Producers . . .Lloyd Shirley, George Taylor
Mr Notting QC . . . . . . .Anthony Dawes	Director . . . . Terry Green
Usher . . . . .Catherine Chase	Executive Producer . . .Verity Lambert

Called for jury service in a case of handling stolen property, Arthur leaves Terry to mind the lockup. Inspector Soames takes over Chisholm's cases while Chisholm is at court as the chief prosecution witness. Terry meets up again with Debbie, who appeared in the first and second seasons. She has now given up stripping and runs a hairdressing and beauty service in which she works directly in the clients' homes. While she is working on one of her clients, two intruders break in, tie up the owner and steal some property. Debbie escapes and calls the police but Soames doubts her story and suspects that she is working with the intruders. When Soames visits Terry at the lockup to investigate Debbie's story he confiscates all the contents for investigation. Arthur, meanwhile, is elected foreman of the jury and, in solidarity with the defendant and to spite Chisholm, does his best to persuade them to return a not guilty verdict in the face of overwhelming evidence.

Episode 36

Season 3/12   First transmission: 31 March 1982

Back in Good Old England
by Andrew Payne

Terry	Dennis Waterman	*Billy*	Norman Beaton
Arthur	George Cole	*The barker*	Jonty Miller
Jack Wragg	Peter Postlethwaite	*Car owner*	Milton Cadman
Archie	David Hargreaves	*Police sergeant*	Stanley McGeagh
Des	George Layton	*Angelis*	George Camiller
Dave	Glynn Edwards	*Detective constable*	Peter Joyce
Painter	John Benfield	*Skipper*	Royston Tickner
McClure	Tony Westrope		
Rycott	Peter Childs		
Old lady	Kathleen St John	Producers	Lloyd Shirley, George Taylor
Chris	Tariq Yanus	Director	Francis Megahy
Neville	Barry McCarthy	Executive Producer	Verity Lambert

Terry's ex-cellmate from the Scrubs, Jack 'Oily' Wragg, appears unexpectedly at the Winchester after three years in Spain where he went on his release from prison. He is loaded with money he claims to have won on the Spanish Lottery. He doesn't reveal that the other members of the gang who went down with him have a score to settle and that he has a hare-brain scheme for another robbery. When he loses all his money, the safest thing for all concerned is for him to go abroad again.

Subplots: The licence on the Winchester Club is up for renewal. Arthur's interest in acquiring property next to a sex shop attracts some unwelcome visitors to the Winchester Club. Arthur has trouble shifting a consignment of 1970s-style flared jeans.

Episode 37

Season 3/13   First transmission: 7 April 1982

In
by Leon Griffiths

Terry	Dennis Waterman	*Rita*	Diane Langton
Arthur	George Cole	*Police doctor*	Dominic Allan
Gypsy Joe	John Hallam	*Escort officer*	David Gretton
Frank McFadden	Brian Cox	*Gary*	Kelvin Omard
Punter	John Rapley	*Georgie*	Barry Stanton
Van radio officer	Brian Grellis	*First heavy*	Simon Watkins
Van driver	Kelvin Spooner	*Billy 'The Ferret'*	Russell Hunter
Inspector Klingmann	Frederick Jaeger	*Nurse*	Annette Badland
Armstrong	Stafford Gordon	*Bridget*	Lindy Whiteford
Rycott	Peter Childs	*Mechanic*	Farrell Sheridan
Armed officer	Timothy Block	*Policeman*	Alan Polonsky
Fingerprint officer	Michael Maynard	*Sergeant*	PJ Davidson
Second officer	Trevor Cooper		
Third officer	Ron Alridge		
Gaoler	Colin Edwynn		
Foreman	Edward Kelsey		
Plain-clothes man	Peter Van Dissel	Producers	Lloyd Shirley, George Taylor
Ronnie	Linal Haft	Director	Ian Toynton
Karen	Debbie Wheeler	Executive Producer	Verity Lambert

When a BMW car that Arthur has just bought is suspected of containing illegal drugs, Rycott takes Arthur in to be questioned by Inspector Kling-mann from Germany who is part of an Anglo-German unit investigating narcotic smuggling. In the absence of Arthur's solicitor, Terry has to track down Frank McFadden, a tough Scot, who sold the car to Arthur and can prove his innocence. By the time Terry traces McFadden, the police can find no sign of the drugs in the car and have to release Arthur, but not before Terry and McFadden get involved in a fight on a London bus which results in Terry being taken in by the police. The stunt fight on the bus platform is particularly impressive.

Episode 38

Season 4/1
First transmission: 26 December 1983

Minder's Christmas Bonus
by Leon Griffiths

Terry . . . . .Dennis Waterman	Producer . . . . George Taylor
Arthur . . . . George Cole	Director . . . . .Ian Toynton
Dave . . . . .Glynn Edwards	Executive Producers . .Verity Lambert,
	. . . . .Lloyd Shirley

Arthur will be spending Christmas by himself because 'er indoors has taken
the kids to Florida to see her brother. Unfortunately, the discount tickets
that Arthur provided turn out to be for stand-by and the family is stranded
at the airport. Arthur, meanwhile, is helping Terry and Dave decorate the
Christmas tree at the Winchester Club in preparation for the Christmas party.
The story is interspersed with clips from episodes 3, 6, 11, 16, 24, 25, 29, 31, 35,
36 and 37.

Episode 39

First transmission: 11 January 1984

Rocky Eight and a Half
by Leon Griffiths

Terry	Dennis Waterman	*Rycott*	Peter Childs
Arthur	George Cole	*Chris*	Peter Kosta
Dave	Glynn Edwards	*Brenda Wilson*	Anna Nygh
Harry Lynch	George Innes	*Darrow*	Frank Gatliff
Nicky	Christine Kavanagh	*Medical official*	Donald Eccles
Soldier Atkins	David Lodge	*Boxing MC*	Jonathan Burn
Referee	Bruce Wells	*Jackie Wilson*	Peter Cheevers
Youth	John Fowler	*Mrs Lynch*	Doreen Keogh
Barman	Brian Calloway		
Cabby	Alex Leppard	Producer	George Taylor
Young lad	Herbert Norville	Director	Ian Toynton
Henry	Joseph Iles	Executive Producers	Verity Lambert,
Eric Morgan	Ian McNeice		Lloyd Shirley

Seven years ago Terry was involved in a rigged boxing bout with Jackie Wilson. Terry was supposed to take a fall after seven rounds. However, he made the fall too obvious and lost his licence. (Arthur considers he should have been nicked for over-acting.) Eric, the promoter, now proposes a return bout with Wilson. Initially unwilling, Terry eventually agrees and goes into training under 'Soldier' Atkins. But then he receives a visit from Wilson's wife Brenda asking him to go easy on Wilson because he has an eye problem and could lose his sight if he fights again. Late in the fight, Terry realises the story is a con and the fight ends in an unexpected way.

Subplot: Arthur is offered a flat for sale after the owner's wife runs off with a double-glazing salesman. Arthur makes money on the fight but finds that he has been the subject of a con trick over the property deal.

Episode 40

Season 4/3   First transmission: 18 January 1984

Senior Citizen Caine
by Andrew Payne

Terry . . . . .Dennis Waterman	*Policeman* . . . . Jonathan Barlow
Arthur . . . . George Cole	*Eddie* . . . . Stan Pretty
Dave . . . . Glynn Edwards	*Bob* . . . . Chris Webb
Cecil Caine . . . . Lionel Jefferies	*Young Scot* . . . . Iain Rattray
Derek Caine . . . . John Carlin	*Jock McLeish* . . . . James Cosmo
Sonia Caine . . . . Susan Fleetwood	*Girls in pub* . . . . Gillian Taylforth,
Johnny Caine . . . . Keith Barron	. . . . Kim Taylforth
Drunk . . . . Griffith Davies	
Christine Caine . . . . Fiona Curzon	
The VAT man . . . . Anthony Hall	Producer . . . . George Taylor
Vicar . . . . Norman Lumsden	Director . . . . Robert Young
Dr Roberts . . . . Kenneth Keeling	Executive Producers . .Verity Lambert,
Sheila Jones . . . . Angela Richards	. . . . Lloyd Shirley

Cecil Caine owns a successful car showroom after working his way up from repairing bicycles in the 1920s. After Cecil's wife dies, he explains to Arthur and Terry that his family is trying to have him committed to a mental hospital so that they can gain control of the business. Cecil escapes from the funeral on his motorbike and finds his way to Terry's place where he hopes to stay while his assistant Miss Jones makes some financial arrangements. He then intends to spend the rest of his life touring Britain's waterways on a narrow boat.

Arthur has acquired some Japanese 'Scotch', and tries to unload some at Jock's Club. Jock insists that Arthur finish a bottle with him. Arthur is unable to stand the pace and passes out when he gets back to his car. He wakes up to find himself in his car being towed to Cecil's son's place where he is put under some pressure to reveal where Cecil is hiding. There is a confrontation on Cecil's narrow boat between the Caine family, Terry, Arthur and the VAT man. And Jock still has a score to settle with Arthur. . . .

Look out for Gillian Taylforth (now well known for her role as Kathy Beale in BBC-1's *EastEnders*) with her sister Kim who have bit parts as girls in a pub.

Episode 41

Season 4/4   First transmission: 25 January 1984

High Drains Pilferer
by Dave Humphries

Terry	Dennis Waterman	Ernie Kestle	Richard Caldicot
Arthur	George Cole	Mandeville	Jeremy Child
Dave	Glynn Edwards	Morris	Keith Smith
Eddie Venables	Chris Matthews	Tucker	TaylorMcAuley
Susie Blake	Sheila Ruskin	Mr Mikabwe	Thomas Baptiste
Micky 'the Fish' Metcalf	David Calder		
DC Jones	Michael Povey		
Chisholm	Patrick Malahide	Producer	George Taylor
Hamster	Paul Brooke	Director	Robert Young
Harbot	Hugh Sullivan	Executive Producers	Verity Lambert,
Laura	Amanda Kemp		Lloyd Shirley

Micky Metcalfe is known as 'the Fish' because of his ability to slide out of trouble. When Micky's girlfriend has her jewellery stolen from her flat while Terry is temporarily driving for him, Terry becomes a suspect. Terry, however, happened to see Eddie, an old cellmate and known cat burglar, in the district on the night of the robbery and suspects him of being involved. On the assumption that the stolen jewellery will find its way into the hands of Ernie Kestle, a local fence, Micky puts some pressure on Kestle to inform him if he gets any information. Arthur, who is now dabbling in the insurance business, devises a scheme for the jewellery to be returned to the insurance company in exchange for the reward money. But unknown to Arthur or Terry, Micky's pressure on Ernie Kestle was effective and the missing jewellery is returned. Arthur discovers that insurance is not something to be taken lightly.

Episode 42

Season 4/5   First transmission: 1 February 1984

Sorry Pal, Wrong Number
by Leon Griffiths

Terry . . . . .Dennis Waterman	*Video man* . . . . Alan Thompson
Arthur . . . . George Cole	*Ernie Grahame* . . . . David Janes
Dave . . . . .Glynn Edwards	*First client* . . . . .Barry Philips
Sprott . . . . Shaun Curry	*Second client* . . . . Chuck Julian
Petal . . . . Jumoke Debayo	*Printer* . . . . .Lee Walker
Railwayman . . . . Timothy Bateson	*Punter* . . . . Alan Chuntz
Fenella . . . . .Rosalind Lloyd	*Nurse* . . . . Caroline Gruber
Andrew . . . . .Royce Mills	*Sylvia* . . . . Angela Wynter
Tony . . . . .Vivian Mann	
Tax inspector . . . . Russel Wootton	
Mo . . . . .Hugh Futcher	Producer . . . . George Taylor
JJ Mooney . . . . TP McKenna	Director . . . . .Terry Green
Car driver . . . . .Richard Wilding	Executive Producers . .Verity Lambert,
Chisholm . . . . Patrick Malahide	. . . . .Lloyd Shirley

Arthur goes into partnership with con man JJ Mooney to sell horseracing selections over the telephone, but first has to find an office with a good postal address and three telephone lines. Arthur solves this by using a postal agency and three public telephone boxes on a railway station, where he persuades the porter to put 'out of order' signs on the boxes between 11 and three o'clock each day in return for a modest retainer. He arranges for Terry to mind the telephone boxes and give out the selections to the clients who ring up. As business increases, Terry recruits Petal, an interested bystander, to help with the calls. However, the business is hampered when the security of the phone boxes is threatened by a juvenile protection racket and when JJ has a heart attack. The business also attracts the interest of Sprott, a disgraced ex-police officer.

Subplot: Arthur has to explain his Jaguar and lockup to the Inland Revenue.

Episode 43

Season 4/6   First transmission: 8 February 1984

The Car Lot Baggers
by Trevor Preston

Terry	Dennis Waterman	*De Ath*	Artro Morris
Arthur	George Cole	*Nathan Loveridge*	Jimmy Nail
Dave	Glynn Edwards	*Ellen*	Chloe Salaman
Cabbie	John Altman	*Landlord*	Eddie Caswell
Mr Rushmer	Christopher Benjamin	*Mrs Murdoch*	June Whitfield
Arnie	Ray Winstone	*Ikey*	Del Baker
Wally	Harry Scott	*Mick*	Jeffrey Stewart
Apsimon	James Faulkner		
Fribbins	Colin Jeavons	Producer	George Taylor
Chisholm	Patrick Malahide	Director	Francis Megahy
Nelson	Martin Anthony	Executive Producers	Verity Lambert,
Harry	Gabriel Kern		Lloyd Shirley

Wally West, a second-hand car dealer friend of Arthur's, has had problems with vandalism on his car lot and asks for Terry's help to mind the lot overnight. Suspicion falls initially on some local gypsies, until Terry befriends one of them and discovers the real vandals and whom they work for. There is a good visual effect when a car is set on fire by one of the vandals and explodes.

Subplots: Arthur is selling second-hand hearses for Mr De Ath, a Welsh undertaker. There is a cameo role for June Whitfield as Mrs Murdoch, the hearse buyer — with more on her mind than buying hearses. Arthur has a car returned with grass growing out of it.

Episode 44

Season 4/7 · First transmission: 15 February 1984

If Money Be The Food of Love, Play On
by Tony Hoare

Terry . . . . .Dennis Waterman	*Keith* . . . . Peter Quince
Arthur . . . . George Cole	*Jim (pub entertainer)* . . . . . . .not credited
Greg Collins . . . . .Larry Lamb	*Ronnie Aldridge* . . . . .Howard Lew Lewis
Dee Rogers . . . . .Penny Downie	*Bobby Finch* . . . . Bernie Searle
Sandra . . . . Julianne White	*Gary Mitchell* . . . . .Keith Bell
Lisa . . . . Sally Tayler	*Builder* . . . . Laurence Harrington
Carp . . . . Patrick Monckton	
Rycott . . . . Peter Childs	
Mournful Maurice . . . . Barry Jackson	*Producer* . . . . George Taylor
Dave . . . . .Glynn Edwards	*Director* . . . . .Terry Green
Boutique assistant . . . .Christine Ellerbeck	*Executive Producers* . .Verity Lambert,
Freddy the Fly . . . . Christopher Driscoll	. . . . .Lloyd Shirley

Arthur becomes captivated by Dee, an attractive young Australian, when she arrives at the Winchester Club seeking his help in locating her fiancé Gary — whom everyone on the manor knows ran off to Australia to escape an arrest warrant. Meanwhile, two Australian shoplifters are operating in the area and are passing their stolen property to Mournful Maurice for disposal. Rycott is keen to establish a connection between Maurice and Arthur. Terry tracks Gary down in London, but the reunion with Dee is far from a happy one.

Episode 45

First transmission: 22 February 1984

A Star is Gorn
by Tony Hoare

Terry	Dennis Waterman		*Cyril Ash*	Mel Smith
Arthur	George Cole		*George*	Tim Healy
Dave	Glynn Edwards		*John Sutton*	Charles Kay
Zac Zolar/Albert Trout/Alan Trent			*Lindsay Browne*	Billy Hamon
	Mike Holoway		*Sarah*	Carrie Jones
Maude Trout	Pearl Hackney		*Jessica Trent*	Jackie Smith-Wood
Melish	Michael Troughton			
Sharon	Primi Townsend		Producer	George Taylor
Rycott	Peter Childs		Director	Ian Toynton
Freddy King	Michael Wynne		Executive Producers	Verity Lambert,
Billy Cronin	Michael Deeks			Lloyd Shirley

When pop star Zac Zolar reportedly dies of a heart attack, Arthur unexpectedly gets hold of a valuable missing master-tape of the singer's last recordings. His attempts to profit from the find are not appreciated by Zac's ex-manager Cyril Ash, and attract the suspicions of Sergeant Rycott, who is already having more trouble than he needs finding someone who can identify Zac's body.

Episode 46

Season 4/9

First transmission: 29 February 1984

Willesden Suite
by Andrew Payne

Terry	. . . . .Dennis Waterman	*Mr Robinson*	. . . . .Brian Hawksley
Arthur	. . . . George Cole	*Sullivan*	. . . . .Peter Sproule
Pongo Harris	. . . . William Simons	*Barry*	. . . . .Valentine Palmer
Sue	. . . . Susan Kyd	*Steve*	. . . . Reece Dinsdale
Norma Bates	. . . . Toby Robins	*Chief Insp Baxter*	. . . . .John Rowe
Father Andrew	. . . . Michael Maloney		
Father Michael	. . . . .John Malcolm		
Karen Bradly	. . . . Sally Jane Jackson	Producer	. . . . George Taylor
Dave	. . . . .Glynn Edwards	Director	. . . . .Francis Megahy
Charles Riding	. . . . Bernard Kay	Executive Producers	. .Verity Lambert,
Philip Higgins	. . . . .Frank Duncan		. . . . .Lloyd Shirley

Arthur is asked to address the Rotary Club at the hotel where Terry is acting as temporary house detective. When the notes to Arthur's speech are stolen, he seeks support from the bottle. Terry has to deal with a teenager hoping to become a photographic model but who has been cheated out of her money, a pair of bogus priests stealing from the guestrooms, and a hotel manager who is handling the proceeds of a jewel robbery. Arthur is selling jam.

Episode 47

Season 4/10   First transmission: 7 March 1984

Windows
by Geoff Case

Terry	Dennis Waterman	*Laura Mancini Allan*	Jenifer Landor
Arthur	George Cole	*Maria-Elaine Allan*	Sara Filek
Dave	Glynn Edwards	*Derek*	Lawrence Lambert
Roddy Allan	Stephen Rea	*Alex*	Alexander Morton
Ms Knight	Judith Byfield	*Billy*	Billy Hartman
Old Irishman	Jack Le White	*Rico*	Mark Lewis
Joe Mancini	Patrick Troughton	*Johnny Petselli*	Tony Anholt
Helena Mancini	Ruth Goring	*Maureen*	Not credited
Marco Mancini	Robert Pereno		
Anthony Mancini	Eddie Mineo	Producer	George Taylor
Janice	Janet Fielding	Director	Robert Young
Linda	Valerie Buchanan	Executive Producers	Verity Lambert,
Louise	Catherine Rabett		Lloyd Shirley

Arthur is planning to open a health club, the 'Daley Workout'. Roddy Allan, who is helping in the venture, is distracted by the disappearance of his Italian wife Laura and their daughter and by rumours that she has gone off with Johnny Petselli. Roddy's relatives set out to seek revenge from Laura's family but inadvertently offend Petselli. It falls on Terry, who is the child's godfather, to negotiate an amicable solution. There are some good visual effects when a road-trenching machine trashes an industrial greenhouse.

Subplot: Arthur is selling telephone answering machines.

Episode 48

Season 4/11   First transmission: 14 March 1984

Get Daley!
by Andrew Payne

Terry . . . . .Dennis Waterman	*Nurse* . . . . Miranda Forbes
Arthur . . . . George Cole	*Dunning* . . . . Harold Goodwin
Dave . . . . .Glynn Edwards	*DC Jones* . . . . .Michael Povey
Keith Wendell . . . . Ian Bartholomew	*Night nurse* . . . . .Janis Winters
Harry Martin . . . . .Frank Mills	*Dr Hills* . . . . .David Hanson
Joe Harrison . . . . Brian Osborne	*Vic Harrison* . . . . Brian Peck
Sammy . . . . Gordon Kaye	*Fowler* . . . . .Richard Warner
Albert Wendell . . . . . . .Roger Hammond	
Dermott . . . . Kevin Lloyd	Producer . . . . George Taylor
Sandra . . . . Maureen O'Farrell	Director . . . . .Ian Toynton
Tony Apsey . . . . .Peter Alexander	Executive Producers . .Verity Lambert,
Chisholm . . . . Patrick Malahide	. . . . .Lloyd Shirley

While finalising a deal with Joe Harrison on some tailors' dummies, Arthur is unwittingly present when a gunman starts threatening Harrison into paying an outstanding gambling debt. The gun accidentally goes off and Harrison dies from a heart attack. As Arthur leaves the warehouse, he is recognised by Harry Martin, the driver of the gunman's getaway car.

Terry's pal Tony, who used to work with Harrison, is a suspect in the case and is taken in for questioning. However, Chisholm learns from an informer that Arthur was around at the time of the shooting and takes a renewed interest in Arthur.

Arthur, meanwhile, has been admitted to hospital for an operation on his ingrowing toenails. His stay is less than peaceful as he receives unsolicited medical advice from a fellow patient and visits from a thug and Chisholm. He learns of a complication with his medical insurance and has to take swift action.

Episode 49

First transmission: 21 March 1984

A Well Fashioned Fit-up
by Barry Purchese

Terry . . . . Dennis Waterman	*Boutique owner* . . . . Jack Chissick
Arthur . . . . George Cole	*Market stallholder* . . . . Richard Ireson
Dave . . . . Glynn Edwards	*Irish fiddler* . . . . Christopher Dunne
Billy . . . . Christopher Fulford	*Eddie* . . . . Sean Lawlor
Nigel . . . . Trevor Steedman	*Colin* . . . . Oengus MacNamara
Kevin O'Hara . . . . Gerard Murphy	*'Giant'* . . . . Bunny Read
Zoe . . . . Sara Sugarman	
Receptionist . . . . .Carole Harrison	
Ronnie Shyvers . . . . . . .Stanley Meadows	Producer . . . . .George Taylor
Fashion buyer . . . . .Fleur Chandler	Director . . . . Jim Hill
Ted . . . . George Little	Executive Producer . . . . Lloyd Shirley

Arthur obtains a consignment of brand-name dresses without labels and tries
to unload some on Ronnie Shyvers, a successful garment distributor. Shyvers
is not interested in the dresses but is interested in having Terry stay in the
showroom overnight for a couple of weeks to mind the collections. Terry,
however, has accepted a job on Saturday night as a bouncer for the opening
of a new Irish pub, The Blarney Stone, and Arthur has to mind the showroom
himself. This presents Arthur with a problem because he has arranged a
meeting at the lockup on Saturday night to store something overnight.
Unable to stand the stress of being alone in the showroom, and anxious to
keep his appointment, Arthur slips out for a while, leaving the showroom
unguarded. While he is away, one of the dress collections is stolen from the
showroom. When Zoe's collection finds its way to the lockup, Arthur and
Terry discover who set up the theft and devise a way of getting back at the
perpetrator.

Episode 50

Season 5/1   First transmission: 5 September 1984

Goodbye Sailor
by Andrew Payne

Terry . . . . .Dennis Waterman	*Secretary* . . . . Sandra Kneller
Arthur . . . . George Cole	*Penny* . . . . Sarah Berger
Dave . . . . Glynn Edwards	*Johnny Winstanley* . . . . . Reginald Marsh
Larry Patel . . . . Rashid Karapiet	*Customs man* . . . . .Derrick Fincham
Arnie . . . . .Ray Winstone	*Antoine* . . . . .Marc Gebhard
Chisholm . . . . Patrick Malahide	*Punter* . . . . Bill Treacher
DC Jones . . . . .Michael Povey	
Van driver . . . . .Freddie Stuart	
Large man . . . . .Peter Rutherford	Producer . . . . George Taylor
Harry Baily . . . . Anthony Langdon	Director . . . . .Francis Megahy
Commander Hawksly . . . . Moray Watson	Executive Producer . . . . .Lloyd Shirley

Arthur does a deal with Commander Hawksly to buy some hand-rolling tobacco smuggled in from the continent. Believing Arthur's claim that the tobacco is unsold stock from Hawksly's tobacconist shop, Terry and Arnie drive down to the coast to collect it while Arthur tries to sell some stolen football boots. When Terry and Arnie arrive at the coast they are told that there is a slight delay and are invited to stay overnight on Hawksly's luxury yacht. But Arthur, horrified to hear that Terry has handed over £2,500 to Hawksly without receiving the goods, drives down to join them overnight. Next morning, Hawksly takes the boat out to meet his French supplier while Arthur, Terry and Arnie are still on board. Only then does Terry discover what he is involved in. After a skirmish with a Customs and Excise vessel, Terry convinces them that they will be unable to get the goods back to shore and that they should dump them over the side. Hawksly's assistant, however, has an idea where the bags may be washed ashore.

Episode 51

Season 5/2 First transmission: 12 September 1984

What Makes Shamy Run?
by Leon Griffiths

Terry	Dennis Waterman	*Indian in pub*	Moti Makan
Arthur	George Cole	*Elderly Indian man*	Ishaq Bux
Dave	Glynn Edwards	*Smudger*	Stacy Davies
Ajit Desal	Albert Moses	*DC Jones*	Michael Povey
Shamy	Art Malik	*Mr Henry*	Robbie Coltrane
Betting shop girl	Francesca Whitburn	*Hotel manager*	Mike McCabe
Syrup	Fred Evans	*Denise*	Chrissie Cotterill
Mr Mitra	Madhav Sharma		
Chisholm	Patrick Malahide	Producer	George Taylor
Gayle	Jacqueline Reddin	Director	Terry Green
Indian housewife	Rani Singh	Executive Producer	Lloyd Shirley

Arthur unknowingly receives a wad of counterfeit £20 notes from Shamy as payment for some dodgy sewing machines. When Arthur innocently uses one of the fake notes at the Winchester Club, Chisholm takes a renewed interest in Terry and Arthur's activities. Terry and Arthur go back to Shamy to redress the issue and discover that he plans to steal the master copy of an Indian movie and take it to India for illegal copying. When the tape is stolen, Arthur receives a visit from a group of Indian heavies intent on getting the tape back.

Subplots: Syrup, who was entrusted with the fake notes at the Winchester uses them to buy a Roger Moore-style wig to replace his outdated Engelbert Humperdinck-style. Arthur has a hair-raising experience as a driving instructor. [N.B. 'syrup of fig': rhyming slang for wig]

Episode 52

Season 5/3   First transmission: 19 September 1984

A Number of Old Wives' Tales
by Tony Hoare

Terry	Dennis Waterman	*Mary*	Kate Williams
Arthur	George Cole	*Chisholm*	Patrick Malahide
Dave	Glynn Edwards	*DC Jones*	Michael Povey
Clive Cosgrove	Patrick Mower	*Man with car*	Bill Moody
Arnie	Ray Winstone	*Barry*	Gary Holton
Mavis	Belinda Sinclair	*Ernie*	Jonathan Kydd
Roland	Kenneth Waller	*Geoffrey*	Peter Dennis
Harry	Michael Attwell	*Kathy*	Sonia Fox
Angie	Vivienne Ritchie		
Peter	David Weston		
Elderly lady	Una Brandon-Jones	Producer	George Taylor
Laura	Sue Holderness	Director	Francis Megahy
Housewife	Su Elliot	Executive Producer	Lloyd Shirley

Clive Cosgrove, who barely knows Terry, asks him to be best man at his wedding. Arthur will be giving away the bride and has promised to provide a Rolls-Royce and a chauffeur. What they don't know is that Clive already has four wives. There is a punch-up at the wedding and they have to use a tow-truck instead of the Rolls-Royce as the bridal car. But when the wives and their relatives start to appear at the Winchester Club in search of Clive, Arthur wishes he had not got involved.

Subplot: Arnie and Terry are collecting wrecked and abandoned cars for scrap.

Episode 53

Season 5/4   First transmission: 26 September 1984

The Second Time Around
by Geoffrey Case

Terry . . . . Dennis Waterman	*Barney Todd* . . . . Bill Maynard
Arthur . . . . George Cole	*John Drayham* . . . . David Webb
Dave . . . . Glynn Edwards	*Faith* . . . . Erika Hoffman
Ronnie Todd . . . . John Landry	*Tony Strong* . . . . Barry Martin
Ruby Hubbard . . . . Beryl Reid	*John Scott* . . . . Peter Birrel
Jane Lugg . . . . Dot Rubin	
Andy . . . . Nigel Le Vaillant	
Temp secretary . . . . . Sara Heliane Elliot	Producer . . . . George Taylor
Susan Hall . . . . Fiona Mollison	Director . . . . Francis Megahy
Jack Hodgson . . . . Ivor Roberts	Executive Producer . . . . Lloyd Shirley

Arthur recently sold a Georgian dining suite for Ronnie Todd, unaware that he was selling it without the knowledge of its real owner, Ruby Hubbard. Ruby, Ronnie's stepmother, was previously a successful writer of romantic novels until she retired to Capri. When Ronnie discovers that Ruby is returning to London to write another novel he asks Arthur to find a replacement for the dining suite. When Ruby returns, Arthur arranges for Terry to keep her company for a few days as she is nervous about living alone in the big house. But she and Terry discover on their return from lunch the following day that the furniture has been cleared out and the house taken over by an obscure religious movement. Ruby realises that her ex-husband Barney and his solicitor have sold the property without her knowledge. Arthur uncovers a conspiracy to defraud Ruby in order to finance a property deal in Spain. He is able to arrange a reconciliation between Barney and Ruby but finds himself with an extra suite of Georgian furniture on his hands.

Episode 54

Season 5/5

First transmission: 10 October 1984

Second Hand Pose

by Tony Hoare

Terry	Dennis Waterman	*Miss Turner*	Ann Morrish
Arthur	George Cole	*Rycott*	Peter Childs
Dave	Glynn Edwards	*Melish*	Michael Troughton
Ambulance attendant	Roger Nott	*Bill*	Ron Boyd
Charlie Pope	Billy Murray	*Ben*	Tim Pearce
Jane	Eileen Nicholas	*Policeman*	Philip Shelley
Roly-Poly Peter	Johnny Shannon		
Mary Tate	Tilly Vosburgh		
Roger Collins	David Warbeck	Producer	George Taylor
Abigail Collins	Stacy Dorning	Director	Roy Ward Baker
John Rawlings	Andrew Lodge	Executive Producer	Lloyd Shirley

After being locked in a meat freezer when one of Arthur's deals goes wrong, Terry decides to find alternative employment. In a rather complex story, Terry teams up with Charlie Pope, a second-hand furniture dealer, to do some general removal work. His first job is to clear a flat for an estate agent after the death of the flat's occupant. Unknown to Terry, however, Pope has actually broken into the flat, and the owner, Miss Turner, is still very much alive. When Terry discovers the deception he persuades Pope to return the stolen furniture to the flat. Miss Turner in the meantime has reported the theft to the police and Rycott takes Terry and Arthur in for questioning. By that time, Miss Turner discovers that her furniture has been returned and Rycott has to release them. Arthur, meanwhile, sells two antique chairs that he bought from Pope but discovers that they were stolen and has to employ two con men to retrieve them.

Subplot: Terry has to mind Roly-Poly Peter, a club owner who is receiving threats for not paying protection money.

Episode 55

The Long Ride Back to Scratchwood
by Leon Griffiths

Terry . . . . Dennis Waterman	*Theo Warren* . . . . David Beale
Arthur . . . . George Cole	*Tax inspector* . . . . Brian Haines
Justin James . . . . Mark Farmer	*Helga* . . . . Annabel Price
Greengrocer . . . . Sydney Golder	*Mechanic* . . . . David Beckett
Joe Eldon . . . . Peter Needham	*Scottish fan* . . . . James Coyle
Steve Benson . . . . Alan Hunter	*Autograph hunter* . . . . Brian Binns
Mario . . . . Nicolas Chagrin	
Phil . . . . James Marcus	
Cedric . . . . Derek Martin	Producer . . . . George Taylor
Alisdair Frazer . . . . Jon Croft	Director . . . . Terry Green
Mrs James . . . . Helen Keating	Executive Producer . . . . Lloyd Shirley

Arthur agrees to finance Justin's scheme to scalp football tickets. Justin's contact, Steve Benson, claims he can get 2,000 tickets for a forthcoming England-Scotland match at face value. The tickets can then be sold to the Scottish fans at a substantial mark-up. Phil the 'ticket king' hears about the scheme and is enraged that he has competition. Meanwhile, Frazer comes down from Scotland to discuss a deal on the tickets with Arthur and insists that Arthur deliver the tickets to Glasgow personally. Phil follows Arthur to Glasgow and, at a stop-off along the way, makes Arthur an offer that he can't refuse for the tickets. Frazer puts an abrupt end to Arthur's deal with Phil when he discovers that the tickets are actually forgeries, and Arthur has to face the fact that he was set up by Benson.

Subplot: Terry is called in to see the tax inspector who has not heard from him for seven years.

Episode 56

Season 5/7   First transmission: 24 October 1984

Hypnotising Rita
by Alan Janes

Terry	Dennis Waterman	*Joany*	June Brown
Arthur	George Cole	*Lady in flat*	Margery Withers
Dave	Glynn Edwards	*Mr Chicory*	Frank Williams
Driver	Michael Redfern	*Clare*	Sally Faulkner
Mr Sharma	Renu Setna	*Mrs Boswell*	Sheila Mathews
Jimmy Elliot	Ray Burdis	*Spriggs*	Charles Rea
Sudbury	Donald Sumpter		
Rita	Nicola Cowper	Producer	George Taylor
Benjy	Tony Calvert	Director	Terry Green
Barney	Vincent Allen	Executive Producer	Lloyd Shirley

While trying to recover an outstanding debt, Arthur and Terry are confronted by Rita and Sudbury, her hypnotist boyfriend, being chased by Rita's brothers. Rita explains that she will inherit some money from her father on her 18th birthday in a few day's time and that her family suspects Sudbury of trying to trick her out of her money. She asks if she can stay with Arthur until her birthday. Terry acts as a mediator between Rita and her mother.

Subplots: Arthur takes over a carpet steam-cleaning business that he calls 'The Daley Help'. He has difficulty shifting 250 litres of brilliant tangerine paint, and discovers that his cigars have a strange taste.

Episode 57

Season 5/8   First transmission: 31 October 1984

The Balance of Power
by David Yallop

Terry . . . . Dennis Waterman	*Taxi driver* . . . . Graham Cull
Arthur . . . . .George Cole	*Woman at door* . . . . Joyce Parry
Dave . . . . Glynn Edwards	*Man with hedge* . . . . Jim Dunk
Macintyre . . . . .Alex McAvoy	*Chisholm* . . . . Patrick Malahide
Julie Waters . . . . Caroline Langrishe	*DC Jones* . . . . Micheal Povey
Commissionaire . . . . Michael Ripper	*Woman with chocolates* . . . . Julie May
Cooke . . . . .Clifford Rose	*Lent* . . . . Peter Woodthorpe
George . . . . Lennard Pearce	
Poker player . . . . Chris Sullivan	
Raymond Wilkins . . . Nicholas Courtney	Producer . . . . .George Taylor
Blakeney . . . . Brian McDermott	Director . . . . Francis Megahy
Rutherford . . . . Neville Jason	Executive Producer . . . . Lloyd Shirley

Arthur discovers that his car lot is the subject of a compulsory purchase order by the local council. He goes to the town hall to protest and learns that his local councillor has died and that the seat is open for re-election. Realising that he could use the position to benefit his own nefarious activities, he stands for election using the platform of 'law and order'. The opposing candidate learns about Arthur's questionable business methods and tries to use this to discredit him. As a result, Terry and Arthur are taken in for questioning following a tip-off that they are involved in a diamond smuggling operation. But Chisholm has to release them when a reporter who is writing about Terry's boxing career threatens to run a story on Chisholm's vendetta against Arthur. The outcome of the election is affected by a supply of chocolates that Arthur wants to shift.

Episode 58

Season 5/9   First transmission: 26 December 1984

Around The Corner
by Tony Hoare

Terry . . . . .Dennis Waterman	*Rycott* . . . . .Peter Childs
Arthur . . . . George Cole	*DC Melish* . . . . .Michael Troughton
Dave . . . . .Glynn Edwards	*Harry* . . . . Sydney Kean
Tasty Tim . . . . Colin Farrell	*Lady in flat* . . . . Joy Lemoine
Fred . . . . Brian Capron	*DI Norton* . . . . Tony Caunter
Ted . . . . Jeff Pirie	
Paddy Hurley . . . . Arthur Whybrow	Producer . . . . George Taylor
Chisholm . . . . Patrick Malahide	Director . . . . Roy Ward Baker
DC Jones . . . . .Michael Povey	Executive Producer . . . . .Lloyd Shirley

Arthur is the victim of a con trick when two contacts of 'Tasty Tim' appear at the Winchester offering a good deal on video players. Rycott and Chisholm have also been fooled into believing that they will be able to catch Arthur red-handed when the video players change hands. When Terry tracks down the con men he not only gets Arthur's money refunded but also manages to work a deal with them to get even with Tasty. As a result, Rycott and Chisholm find themselves victims of yet another hoax.

Subplot: Arthur acquires a greyhound that he intends to race at White City but the dog refuses to run. Arthur cannot bring himself to smear mustard over its 'nether region' as recommended by the seller.

Episode 59

Season 6/1   First transmission: 4 September 1985

Give Us This Day Arthur Daley's Bread
by Andrew Payne

Terry . . . . Dennis Waterman	*Fiona* . . . . Geraldine Alexander
Arthur . . . . George Cole	*Chisholm* . . . . Patrick Malahide
Dave . . . . Glynn Edwards	*DC Jones* . . . . Micheal Povey
Mrs Bickerton Jones . . . . Avril Elgar	*Mrs Foskitt* . . . . Patsy Smart
Mr Howlett . . . . Ellis Dale	*First policeman* . . . . .Roger Tallon
Marion . . . . David Jackson	*Second policeman* . . . . . . .David Landberg
Glue . . . . Eric Francis	*Ron* . . . . .Paul Cooper
Paper . . . . .Nat Jackley	
Vincent . . . . David Jessiman	
Godfrey . . . . James Booth	Producer . . . . .George Taylor
Reverend Redwood . . . . . .Norman Eshley	Director . . . . Francis Megahy
Mrs Hurst . . . . Sylvia Kay	Executive Producer . . . . Lloyd Shirley

Arthur offers work as landscape gardeners to a motley group of ex-prisoners who meet periodically at the local church under the supervision of the Reverend Redwood. The group is led by Godfrey, who wears teddy-boy jackets and has a fondness for the expression 'blah, blah, blah — b'boom'. The appearance of the gardeners in the area coincides with a spate of robberies and house-breakings. Chisholm, who is being pressured by his superiors to stamp it out, tries to warn Arthur's client that the gardeners pose a serious risk but she is a woman of strong principles and refuses to stop the work. Chisholm then gets a tip-off that stolen property is being stored in the church. Godfrey and his crew have to work fast to dispose of the stolen goods.

Subplots: Arthur gets a phone call from God, Jones has to decide whether he is a Welshman or a policeman, and he and Chisholm get arrested.

Episode 60

Season 6/2   First transmission: 11 September 1985

Life in the Fast Food Lane
by Alistair Beaton

Terry . . . . .Dennis Waterman	*Chisholm* . . . . .Patrick Malahide
Arthur . . . . George Cole	*DC Jones* . . . . .Michael Povey
Dave . . . . .Glynn Edwards	*Heavy* . . . . .Peter Brayham
McTaggart . . . . .Jake D'Arcy	*Doctor* . . . . Benjamin Whitrow
Sarah Bates . . . . .Jan Francis	*Hotel detective* . . . . .Bernard Taylor
Ozzie . . . . Peter Capaldi	*Julie* . . . . Debbie Arnold
Private detective . . . . . . .Howard Attfield	*First prostitute* . . . . .Annee Blott
Granger . . . . Timothy Carlton	*Second prostitute* . . . . .Cate Fowler
Cedric . . . . .James Duggan	*Andrew* . . . . .Royce Mills
Shop assistant . . . . .Melanie Hughes	
Sir Ronald Bates . . . . .David Daker	Producer . . . . George Taylor
Marketing man . . . . James Griffiths	Director . . . . .Terry Green
Sir Ronald's secretary . . . . . . Emma Shaw	Executive Producer . . . . .Lloyd Shirley

Arthur buys a job lot of car phones but discovers they are not compatible with the British telephone system. Assured that all that the phones need to become compatible is a green sticker, Arthur and Terry set about obtaining some stickers from a telephone shop. Terry, meanwhile, has established a relationship with Sarah Bates, the daughter of Sir Ronald Bates, a self-made business tycoon who has worked his way up from the slums and now controls a successful fast-food chain. Sarah's father finds out about her relationship with Terry and sends some thugs to Terry's flat to warn him off. Spotting an opportunity for easy money, Arthur does a deal with Bates to collect £10,000 if he can guarantee that Terry will stop seeing Sarah. To achieve this Arthur has to endure a delicate consultation with his doctor and the embarrassment of a chance meeting with his accountant after having engaged the services of a prostitute for the night. Terry's relationship with Sarah comes to an end without Arthur's intervention, but Arthur discovers that he has no chance of claiming the cash. Arthur discovers what a *barmpot* is.

Episode 61

Season 6/3   First transmission: 18 September 1985

The Return of the Invincible Man
by Leon Griffiths

Terry . . . . Dennis Waterman	*Chisholm* . . . . Patrick Malahide
Arthur . . . . George Cole	*Nurse* . . . . Shevaun Bryers
Dave . . . . Glynn Edwards	*Margaret Stuart* . . . . Anne Kristen
Angie . . . . .Anna Savva	*DC Jones* . . . . Michael Povey
Solly Salmon . . . . John Bluthal	*Doctor* . . . . David Shaughnessy
Painter . . . . .Pat Roach	*Ward Sister* . . . . .Cleo Sylvestre
Ron . . . . .Paul Cooper	
Billy Beesley . . . . Michael Sarne	Producer . . . . .George Taylor
Benny Beesley . . . . .David Shawyer	Director . . . . .Roy Ward Baker
Scotch Harry . . . . .Phil McCall	Executive Producer . . . . Lloyd Shirley

Solly Salmon offers Arthur £3,000 to arrange for his safe to be blown so he can claim that the redundancy pay due to his ex-employees has been stolen. Arthur draws upon the services of Scotch Harry, who was released from prison a few hours earlier, to do the job with the assistance of the incompetent Beezley brothers. Harry (previously seen in Episode 3) is injured when the blast goes wrong and the Beezleys dump him back in Arthur's care. Terry and Arthur try to get Harry into hospital without their being seen but Terry is recognised by a nurse. Terry is taken in for questioning as a suspect for the safe job but has to be released when Chisholm discovers that he can personally provide Terry with an alibi. Concerned that Harry will be recognised by the police when the bandages are removed from his face, Arthur and Terry remove Harry from the hospital and return him to his wife on whom he walked out several years ago. Marital harmony is restored but Arthur finds himself out of pocket.

Episode 62

Season 6/4   First transmission: 25 September 1985

Arthur is Dead, Long Live Arthur
by Tony Hoare

Terry	Dennis Waterman	*Ron*	Paul Cooper
Arthur	George Cole	*Chisholm*	Patrick Malahide
Dave	Glynn Edwards	*DC Jones*	Michael Povey
Andrew	Royce Mills	*Daphne Mount*	Penny Morrell
Justin	Mark Farmer	*Mr Granger*	Jon Laurimore
Freddy the Fly	Robert Austin	*First reporter*	Barry Ewart
Undertaker	Timothy Kightley	*Second reporter*	John Livesey
Mr Muir	Jonathan Elsom		
John Beadle	John Alkin	Producer	George Taylor
Second-hand Sid	Ben Howard	Director	Terry Green
Albert	Johnny Wade	Executive Producer	Lloyd Shirley

Arthur fakes his suicide when he is unable to bring himself to pay a £20,000 tax bill. He hides out at a hotel run by a lonely widow, Mrs Mount, and keeps in touch with Terry with instructions on how to deal with his ongoing business interests. His fake suicide note, blaming the tax system and police harassment for his demise, is discovered by a reporter who runs a story about his disappearance. Few people, however, especially his creditors and Chisholm, take his disappearance seriously. Arthur's morale is lowered still further when he discovers that his assets are frozen pending probate, his lockup has been broken into by creditors, and that 'er indoors has put their flat up for sale and has started selling cars at bargain prices from the car lot. When the hotel owner recognises Arthur's photograph in a newspaper article and becomes too demanding for Arthur's comfort, he is forced to collude with Mrs Mount to make an honourable and convincing reappearance.

Penny Morell, who plays Mrs Mount in this episode, is George Cole's wife in real life.

Episode 63

From Fulham with Love
by Tony Hoare

Terry . . . . Dennis Waterman	*1st Russian crewman* . . . . .Peter Majer
Arthur . . . . .George Cole	*2nd Russian crewman* . . . . David Marrick
Dave . . . . Glynn Edwards	*Vladimir* . . . . .Alexei Jawdokimov
Micky Coyne . . . . .Richard Piper	*Ronnie* . . . . Bill Thomas
Ernie . . . . Joe Melia	*Bank teller* . . . . .April Walker
Captain . . . . .Czeslaw Grocholski	*Police sergeant* . . . . Paul Haley
Sergei . . . . .Michael Gothard	*Chief Insp Norton* . . . . . . .Tony Caunter
Nigel . . . . Jonathan Warren	*Nigel's mum* . . . . .Claire Davenport
Natasha . . . . .Rula Lenska	
Lubov . . . . Mitzi Mueller	Producer . . . . .George Taylor
Chisholm . . . . .Patrick Malahide	Director . . . . Francis Megahy
DC Jones . . . . Michael Povey	Executive Producer . . . . Lloyd Shirley

Through his contact, Ernie, Arthur is selling tracksuits and Walkmans to the crew of a Russian ship that is in port. He receives payment in roubles but later discovers that these cannot be exchanged through the British banking system. Ernie, meanwhile, takes one of the crewmen out to the West End and there is fear that he may try to defect. Natasha, the ship's attractive bosun, appears at Terry's flat to ask for his help in getting the missing crewman back. Arthur sees this as a way of getting his roubles exchanged.

Chisholm is investigating some questionable watches that have started to circulate on the manor. He questions Arthur's skinhead nephew Nigel who is temporarily working for Arthur and learns about Arthur's deal with the Russians. Chisholm arrives on the scene just as Arthur is handing the missing crewman back to Natasha and narrowly avoids a diplomatic incident when he takes them all in for questioning.

Episode 64

Season 6/6   First transmission: 9 October 1985

Waiting For Goddard
by Leon Griffiths

Terry	. . . . .Dennis Waterman	*Albert Goddard*	. . . . Ronald Fraser
Arthur	. . . . George Cole	*Scooter*	. . . . .Kenneth Cope
Dave	. . . . .Glynn Edwards	*Georgie*	. . . . Dimitri Andreas
Bank teller	. . . . .Hilary Gish	*Mr Prosser*	. . . . Donald Douglas
Bank manager	. . . . .Douglas Milvain	*Irishman*	. . . . . Christopher Whitehouse
Mugger	. . . . Sean Barrett		
Chisholm	. . . . Patrick Malahide	Producer	. . . . George Taylor
DC Jones	. . . . .Michael Povey	Director	. . . . Roy Ward Baker
Caroline Selby	. . . . .Mel Martin	Executive Producer	. . . . .Lloyd Shirley

Arthur receives a visit from a private investigator Miss Selby who is trying to contact an eccentric elderly recluse, Albert Goddard, who may have inherited a fortune. If Arthur can locate him he will receive a finder's fee. But Arthur is more interested in becoming Goddard's agent and receiving a percentage of the inheritance. Against Terry's wishes they manage to track down Goddard at his shack and Arthur persuades him to move into one Arthur's rental properties until he has made the arrangements for Goddard to meet the solicitor, Mr Prosser. The solicitor, however, suspects that Arthur is holding Goddard against his will and asks for Chisholm's help.

Subplots: Arthur and Terry fall out after Arthur is mugged and has his briefcase stolen without Terry there to protect him. Arthur's supplier Scooter acquires some suit material for Arthur, delivers a sofa to Arthur in a Harrods van and sells Dave what he claims is a Cartier watch. Chisholm is measured for a suit but discovers that the material he wants to use has been stolen from the tailor who is measuring him. Arthur tries to use Luncheon Vouchers in the Winchester. There is a cliffhanger at the end of the episode, the last in the season, when we see Terry walking out on Arthur again.

Episode 65

Christmas special   First transmission: 25 December 1985

Minder on the Orient Express
by *Andrew Payne*

Arthur . . . . .George Cole	*Car lot customer* . . . . David Beale
Terry . . . . Dennis Waterman	*Hooray Henry* . . . . .Richard Linford
Dave . . . . Glynn Edwards	*Kurt Wengler* . . . . Hans Meyer
Jack South . . . . John Hartley	*Karen Wengler* . . . . Katja Kersten
Young Nikki . . . . .Alexandra Avery	*Helen Spender* . . . . Honor Blackman
Deborah South . . . . .Katharine Schofield	*Ted Moore* . . . . .James Faulkner
Bozz Boswell . . . . .Arthur Whybrow	*Debbie Moore* . . . . Virginia Wetherall
Browning . . . . Karl Howman	*Harry Ridler* . . . . .Ronald Lacey
Pope . . . . .Jesse Birdsall	*Angelo Cappelloni* . . . Manning Redwood
Brian Gamage . . . . Linal Haft	*Angelo's girlfriend* . . . . . . .Debbie Arnold
Van driver . . . . .Jonathan Kydd	*Meredith Gascoyne* . . . .Maurice Denham
Annie . . . . Linda Hayden	*The Judge* . . . . .Robert Beatty
Bank official . . . . Frank Duncan	*English waiter* . . . . .Roger Tallon
Nikki South . . . . Amanda Pays	*François LeBlanc* . . . . Ralph Bates
Mr Dryden . . . . .Dennis Edwards	*Judge's wife* . . . . Helen Horton
James Crane . . . . Adam Faith	*Chef de train* . . . . John Serret
Barry Hart . . . . .Patrick Field	*Claude* . . . . John Moreno
Mark Graves . . . . James Coombes	*French waiter* . . . . Colin Vancao
Chisholm . . . . Patrick Malahide	*French chef* . . . . .Daniel Rovai
DC Jones . . . . Michael Povey	
Rycott . . . . .Peter Childs	
DC Melish . . . . Michael Troughton	Producer . . . . .George Taylor
Police constable . . . . .Milton Cadman	Director . . . . Francis Megahy
Supt Mason . . . . Garfield Morgan	Executive Producer . . . . Lloyd Shirley

'I've never really rated trains: screaming kids, skinheads and sandwiches, karsi awash.' So says Arthur Daley as he and Terry prepare for a few days of luxury on the Orient Express bound for the continent.

In this, the first of two full-length *Minder* feature films, Terry intervenes to prevent a young heiress, Nikki, from being mugged outside the London club he is minding and she rewards him with two tickets for the Orient Express. He intends to take his girlfriend Annie on the trip but finds Arthur waiting for him at the station instead after tricking Annie into parting with her ticket. Terry soon discovers that Nikki is also on the train having asked him along to protect her from a vicious gang who are after her inheritance. He also discovers that the inheritance is actually the proceeds of a bullion robbery masterminded years ago by Nikki's late father who stashed it away in a Swiss bank. Unknown to any of them, Chisholm is also on the train liaising with François LeBlanc, a French detective from Interpol, to keep surveillance on the gang members. Completely out of his depth, Chisholm's attempts to blend in with his cool Interpol counterpart (superbly played by Ralph Bates) are priceless.

Andrew Payne's clever story line has all the hallmarks of the Agatha Christie original, incorporating a mixed collection of well-to-do characters amidst the trappings of luxury travel. There is a judge (played by Robert Beatty), a wealthy socialite (Honor Blackman), a pickpocket, Arthur as the mistaken target of a gangland hit contract, and a gang chasing after the robbery proceeds. Former pop idol Adam Faith is delightfully miscast as a hard nut, gun-toting villain. Dennis Waterman later described his initial misgivings at having to appear frightened of Adam Faith's character. He told director Francis Megahy that he didn't think the idea would work: 'I've got two daughters who are bigger than him!'

But this was *Minder* at the peak of its success. Money was no object and the film took a month to make, including 10 days on location in Boulogne. The film was a huge success.

Episode 66

Christmas special · · · · · · · · · · · · · · First transmission: 26 December 1988

An Officer and a Car Salesman
by Tony Hoare

Arthur	George Cole	Rycott	Peter Childs
Terry	Dennis Waterman	Alfie	George Sweeney
Dave	Glynn Edwards	Cooper	Gary Raynsford
Prison gatekeeper	Jim Dunk	Mitchell	Nigel Miles-Thomas
Dixon	Mark McManus	Casey (Musket One)	Bill Leadbitter
Roger	Simon Williams	Refinery manager	Gordon Salkilld
Williams	John Judd	Security guards	Martin Fisk, Sean Blowers
Caplan	Richard Briers	Asst commissioner	Timothy Carlton
Angie	Diana Quick	Police officer	Iain Rattray
Chisholm	Patrick Malahide		
DC Jones	Michael Povey		
Bindle	Al Ashton	Producer	George Taylor
Chisholm's boss	Clive Swift	Director	Roy Ward Baker
Supt Mason	Garfield Morgan	Executive Producer	John Hambley

Terry is released from an 18-month prison sentence for robbery after Arthur stashed a load of stolen videos in his flat without his knowledge. Arthur, in the meantime, has built up an impressive import-export business and is driving a Rolls-Royce. Chisholm has now resigned from the force after an enquiry board into his paranoia about Arthur's activities and is now chief security officer at a private security firm.

Arthur is asked to supply military equipment to Colonel Caplan who runs a military-style executive survival course. Unknown to Arthur he is also planning to ambush a convoy transporting gold bars. Chisholm is organising security for the convoy, unaware that one of his staff is leaking details of the operation to the Colonel.

Terry wants nothing to do with Arthur on his release and gets a job as a handyman at Caplan's estate. While on an errand for Caplan he finds himself captured by Caplan's men along with Arthur, Rycott, and Jones to ensure that they do not impede the gold ambush which is about to take place.

Episode 67

Season 7/1   First transmission: 2 January 1989

It's a Sorry Lorry, Morrie
by Tony Hoare

Terry	Dennis Waterman	*Fat Charlie*	Roy Kinnear
Arthur	George Cole	*Police constable*	Stephen Gray
Dave	Glynn Edwards	*Punter*	Charles Baillie
Bertie	Terry John	*Supt Mason*	Garfield Morgan
Mickey	Steve McFadden	*Harry*	Thomas Kett
George	Ken Farrington	*Launderette lady*	Catrina Hylton-Hull
Self-inflicted Sid	Ronald Fraser	*Teenager*	Chris Pitt
DS Jones	Michael Povey	*Keith*	Tom Owen
MacDonald	Robin Cameron	*Young mother*	Claire Toeman
Justin	Mark Farmer	*Peter*	Aaron Mason
Morrie	James Marcus		
DS Rycott	Peter Childs	Producer	George Taylor
DC Mellish	Michael Troughton	Director	Roy Ward Baker
Park keeper	Michael Stainton	Executive Producer	John Hambley

Arthur's business is bad. The shelves in his lockup are bare and he has second-hand cars parked along the street while he searches for another car lot. Temptation gets the better of him when Justin tells him about a lorry-load of stolen electrical goods looking for a buyer. Not knowing that the goods are stolen, Terry agrees to drive the lorry to Arthur's new car lot. When he discovers that the police are investigating the lorry he realises that he is implicated in the crime and that his fingerprints will be on the lorry. They call upon the services of 'Self-inflicted Sid' to dispose of the evidence.

Episode 68

Season 7/2 First transmission: 9 January 1989

Days of Fines and Closures
by David Yallop

Terry	Dennis Waterman	MacDonald	Robin Cameron
Arthur	George Cole	Dave's neighbour	Thelma Ruby
Justin	Mark Farmer	William Shanks	John Nettleton
Dave	Glynn Edwards	Magistrate	Thorley Walters
Auctioneer	Tim Barrett	Muldoon	Tony Selby
Rival bidder	Paul Gregory	Magistrate	Mary Law
Tony Benson	Johnny Shannon	Police solicitor	Constantine Gregory
Tombo	Del Henney	Lucy Harris	Patricia Maynard
Fletcher	Michael Melia		
Cooper	George Baker		
Reggie	Colin Prockter	Producer	George Taylor
Rycott	Peter Childs	Director	William Brayne
Jones	Michael Povey	Executive Producer	John Hambley

Terry finds himself minding the Winchester Club when Dave fails to return after a day trip to Folkestone. The appearance of Cooper and his two heavies at the club demanding £2,000 owed by Dave adds a sinister side to Dave's disappearance. Terry, as the club's representative in Dave's absence, has to attend court to apply for the club's licence renewal. Rycott objects on the grounds that it is a meeting place for petty villains. Jones on the other hand prefers to support the application to keep the villains in one place. With Dave's solicitor temporarily called away, Arthur, acting on inside information, successfully counters Rycott's objection and gets himself made the licensee. Dave is not quite prepared for what he finds on his return to the Winchester.

Subplots: Justin becomes a temporary bouncer. Jones does a good turn for Arthur, and Arthur repays it when the heavies set out to recover Dave's debt. Dave's wife, Lucy (played by Dennis Waterman's wife Patricia Maynard), makes an appearance.

Episode 69

Season 7/3   First transmission: 16 January 1989

Fatal Impression
by Anita Bronson

Terry	Dennis Waterman	*Devla*	Valerie Lilley
Arthur	George Cole	*Woman mourner*	Pamela Cundell
Dave	Glynn Edwards	*Dermot*	David Adair
Larchlap Riley	Dick Sullivan	*Mr Marsden*	John Abineri
Sylvie	Kim Thomson	*Newspaper reporter*	Anwen Rees
Little Steve	Stephen Cuttle	*Stevo*	Ian Redford
Tick Tack	Billy Connolly		
Detective	Steven Law	Producer	George Taylor
Pub singer	Sheila Steafel	Director	Terry Green
Pianist	Paul McGuire	Executive Producer	John Hambley

When Arthur's business contact, Larchlap Riley, a reformed gambler, dies owing him money, Arthur discovers that he is not the only person waiting for compensation. Riley does leave behind the sheet he died on, bearing his imprint, which Arthur believes can bring him money as a sacred artefact. Terry lends a helping hand to an old friend who turns up on his doorstep with her two children after being beaten up by her husband. Much to Arthur's dismay, Terry decides it is time to settle down and apply for a job.

Episode 70

First transmission: 23 January 1989

The Last Video Show
by Andrew Payne

Terry	Dennis Waterman	*Charlie*	David Arlen
Arthur	George Cole	*Sinclair*	Milton Johns
Dave	Glynn Edwards	*Customer*	Lee Walker
Jack Last	Ian McShane	*Seedy customer*	Ken Campbell
Sandra Last	Rula Lenska	*Simon*	Jasper Jacob
Freddie Dyer	Brian Blessed	*Rycott*	Peter Childs
Sergeant Bradshaw	Tony Vogel	*Melish*	Michael Troughton
Arnie	Ray Winstone	*Supt Mason*	Garfield Morgan
Duncan	Anthony Corriette		
Nigel	Patrick Ryecart		
Martin	Fraser Downie	Producer	George Taylor
Plain-clothes officer	Paul Beringer	Director	Roy Ward Baker
Tracy	Emma Wray	Executive Producer	John Hambley

While Terry is minding Arthur's new videotape rental business, he comes into possession of a video of a known criminal and a senior police officer in a compromising situation. Arthur realises that the tape could become useful in the future. In the meantime he is doing a good trade receiving second-hand building materials from Arnie and selling them to a local architect. Rycott sees his chance to finally pin something on Arthur when a witness identifies Arnie as the person who stole building items from his site.

Episode 71

Season 7/5   First transmission: 30 January 1989

Fiddler on the Hoof
by David Humphries

Terry . . . . .Dennis Waterman	*Shop assistant* . . . . John Tordoff
Arthur . . . . George Cole	*George Lynch* . . . . Peter Quince
Dave . . . . .Glynn Edwards	*Imogen* . . . . Carole Ashby
Car lot punter . . . . Clem Davis	*Café proprietor* . . . . Gerald Campion
Maltese Tony . . . . Michael Kitchen	*Mr Kramer's man* . . . . . . Lloyd McGuire
Assistant manager . . . . .David Simeon	*Hotel receptionist* . . . . Debbie Roza
TV reporter . . . . April Walker	
Dez . . . . Trevor Thomas	Producer . . . . George Taylor
Billy Lynch . . . . Don Henderson	Director . . . . .Terry Green
Mick . . . . Billy Murray	Executive Producer . . . .John Hambley

A chance meeting between Arthur and Maltese Tony is captured in a TV news report and alerts Billy Lynch of Tony's return to England after a period overseas. Lynch has a score to settle with Tony following the imprisonment of Lynch's brother for an offence in which Tony was involved but escaped prosecution. Lynch wrongly suspects that Arthur knows of Tony's whereabouts and puts pressure on him to reveal the information. Arthur, meanwhile, is preoccupied with the security of £25,000 in cash that he has recovered from his safe deposit box.

[N.B. 'On the hoof': moving from one place to another]

Episode 72

Season 7/6   First transmission: 6 February 1989

The Wrong Goodbye
by David Yallop

Terry	Dennis Waterman	*Jones*	Michael Povey
Arthur	George Cole	*Car salesman*	Richard Linford
Dave	Glynn Edwards	*Andrew*	Royce Mills
Billy	Ray Mort	*Muir*	Jonathan Elsom
William Pierce	Simon Cadell	*Bus driver*	Jonty Miller
Guy Wheeler	Paul Eddington	*Woman on bus*	Una Brandon-Jones
Tony Davis	Michael Lees	*DHSS manager*	Morris Perry
Bernard McKenna	Iain Cuthbertson		
Veronica	Cassie Stuart		
Justin	Mark Farmer	Producer	George Taylor
Melish	Michael Troughton	Director	Francis Megahy
Rycott	Peter Childs	Executive Producer	John Hambley

Arthur can't get credit at the Winchester Club, his bank manager bounces his cheques, and he is served with a summons for the repayment of outstanding debts. But all his problems seem to be solved when a property developer makes an offer on his lockup and car lot. Arthur starts to plan his retirement.

Subplots: Melish's car is involved in a collision with Terry's. Arthur is selling talking dolls, and he enquires about a retirement pension from the DHSS.

This was the last appearance of Peter Childs as Detective Sergeant Rycott. Sadly, he died later that year.

Episode 73

First transmission: 5 September 1991

The Loneliness of the Long Distance Entrepreneur
by David A. Yallop

Arthur	George Cole	*Pat Norris*	Roberta Taylor
Ray	Gary Webster	*Morry*	Raymond Brody
Dave	Glynn Edwards	*Ginger Blythe*	Albie Woodington
DS Morley	Nicholas Day	*Wilf*	Tim Barker
DC Park	Stephen Tompkinson	*Anton*	Philippe Smolikowsky
Pierre	Vania Vilers		
Doreen Daley	Lill Roughley	Producer	Ian Toynton
Bert Daley	Sidney Livingstone	Director	Diarmuid Lawrence
Lucy	Allie Byrne	Executive Producer	John Hambley

Arthur's business is booming and he is now running a successful company (Daley into Europe Ltd) importing used cars from Brussels. But when he discovers that Terry has got married and gone to Australia he urgently needs to find a new assistant. Reluctantly, he employs his nephew Ray and begins to regret it almost immediately. On his first morning, Ray breaks into the lockup, lets two cars and a dozen video players go without taking cash, and accepts a cheque from 'Bouncing Morry'. However, when a pair of heavies starts to threaten Dave over protection money, Ray shows he is able to handle himself and Arthur decides to take him on as his new minder. Meanwhile, Arthur's supplier on the continent insists on road-testing every car he supplies before releasing it to Arthur. Arthur and Ray realise that there may be something valuable hidden in the cars and would like to examine the most recent import. But Arthur has sold it to DS Morley — and he is reluctant to part with it.

Episode 74

Season 8/2   First transmission: 12 September 1991

A Bouquet of Barbed Wine
by Kevin Sperring and Bernard Dempsey

Arthur . . . . .George Cole	Miss Fuller . . . . .Julia St John
Ray . . . . Gary Webster	Dental receptionist . . . . . Helena Lymberg
Dave . . . . Glynn Edwards	Policeman . . . . Martyn Read
DS Morley . . . . .Nicholas Day	Model . . . . .Sophie Heyman
DC Park . . . . Stephen Tompkinson	Theo . . . . .Peter Godwin
Collins . . . . Philip McGough	
Gloria . . . . Emma Cunningham	Producer . . . . Ian Toynton
Parnham . . . . Charlie Roe	Director . . . . .Diarmuid Lawrence
Artemis . . . . Dimitri Andreas	Executive Producer . . . John Hambley

Arthur buys a job lot of wine, allegedly made by the Brothers of the Blessed Bidolph ('a small monastic order off the A2'), and arranges to launch it as a new British wine. When the wine is locked in a warehouse after the supplier is taken in for police questioning, Arthur and Ray have to find a way to get it out in time for the launch. But having got it out, Arthur discovers that the whole consignment is corked. He needs to return it to the warehouse before it is missed so that he can claim a refund. Things go wrong and Arthur is left hanging in the lift well overnight.

Subplot: Arthur visits the dentist and is affected by the anaesthetic. Ray prepares for the photo shoot of a commercial in which he is supposed to appear.

Episode 75

Season 8/3   First transmission: 19 September 1991

Whatever Happened to Her Indoors
by David A. Yallop

Arthur	George Cole	*Drummond*	Richard Syms
Ray	Gary Webster	*Magistrate*	Geraldine Newman
Dave	Glynn Edwards	*Greg Hunter*	Philip Glenister
DS Morley	Nicholas Day	*Photographer*	Phillip Reader
DC Park	Stephen Tompkinson	*Neighbour*	Wilfred Grove
Richards	Kevin McNally	*Traffic policeman*	Jonathan Donne
Doreen Daley	Lill Roughley		
Billy	George Costigan		
Bert Daley	Sidney Livingstone	Producer	Ian Toynton
Lynn	Cherry Gillespie	Director	Roger Bamford
Andrew Shanks	Michael Garner	Executive Producer	John Hambley

Arthur has to defend himself in court when he disregards a council order to remove a British flag emblazoned with the words BRITISH IS BEST from the car lot. Morley, meanwhile, receives information suggesting that Mrs Daley has disappeared and begins to suspect Arthur of a serious crime. His suspicions are heightened when he discovers that Arthur has a large insurance policy on his wife's life and that he is currently suffering a major cash flow problem. Concerned that the police investigation will lead to a search of the lockup, Arthur sets about clearing his stock.

Subplot: Arthur is selling musical timers, and a reporter wants to do a story about Arthur's patriotism.

Episode 76

Season 8/4   First transmission: 26 September 1991

Three Cons Make a Mountain
by David A. Yallop

Arthur	George Cole	*Middleton*	Peter Craze
Ray	Gary Webster	*Steve*	Barry McCarthy
Dave	Glynn Edwards	*Roger*	Gary Powell
DS Morley	Nicholas Day	*Mark*	Howard Ward
DC Park	Stephen Tompkinson	*Frank Wilson*	Nick Kemp
Ashley Brown	David Ryall	*Mr Fletcher*	David Jackson
Nick Rutherford	Dermot Crowley	*Auction assistant*	Jonny Lee Miller
Lucie	Allie Byrne		
Big Mike	Geoffrey Greenhill	Producer	Ian Toynton
Auctioneer	Terence Harvey	Director	Mike Vardy
Morry	Raymond Brody	Executive Producer	John Hambley

Arthur finds himself on the receiving end of con tricks set up by three small-time villains he has got the better of over the years. He finds himself landed with a cheap East German car when he was expecting a luxury vehicle; he buys a lame greyhound at auction, believing that he was bidding for furniture; and he is persuaded to buy a valuable upright piano, only to find that it is worth only £100. But things are not as bad as they seem. He installs the piano in the Winchester Club (and gives a rendition of *I Did it My Way*), the greyhound can be used for breeding, and Ray manages to set up his own con on the people who conned Arthur and makes a profit from them on the car.

Episode 77

Season 8/5   First transmission: 3 October 1991

Guess Who's Coming to Pinner
by David A. Yallop

Arthur	George Cole	*Jeff*	Shaun Curry
Ray	Gary Webster	*Landlord*	Robert Hamilton
Dave	Glynn Edwards	*Station officer*	Hugh Armstrong
DS Morley	Nicholas Day	*Vicar*	Neville Phillips
DC Park	Stephen Tompkinson	*CID officers*	Brendan O'Hea, Luke Sibley
The Widow Johnson	Susan Tracy	*Reporter*	Daniel Mitchell
Tommy Hambury	Michael Gambon	*Man in pub*	Mark Hopkins
Supt Copeland	John Rowe	*Delivery driver*	Michael Pallant
DS Cody	Dorian Healy		
Joanna	Gina McKee	Producer	Ian Toynton
Melville	Hugh Dickson	Director	Diarmuid Lawrence
Alan Kelross	Toby Salaman	Executive Producer	John Hambley

Arthur meets up with Tommy Hambury, a big-time villain he once knew, while attending the funeral of another high-profile villain on the manor. During the wake, Hambury tries to interest Arthur in his next big job, but Arthur has too much to drink and cannot remember any details. When he starts to receive mysterious deliveries paid for by Hambury, Arthur realises that he is involved in a major crime but has no idea what he has agreed to. Even Morley and his superiors are baffled by Arthur's sudden association with the big league. Arthur therefore sets out to regain some recollection of what happened at the wake. He can't contact Hambury; the widow has worrying ideas about being more than just a friend to Arthur; and his idea of getting drunk to try to recall what happened only makes things worse. Even a Harley Street specialist cannot help. But Hambury finally makes contact and arranges a midnight meeting on Southend Pier....

Subplot: Ray finds a new girlfriend, unaware of her true identity.

Episode 78

Season 8/6   First transmission: 10 October 1991

The Last Temptation of Daley
by William Ivory

Arthur	George Cole	*Policeman*	Keith Osborn
Ray	Gary Webster	*Checkout girl*	Faith Edwards
Dave	Glynn Edwards	*Winchester customer*	Christopher Mitchell
DS Morley	Nicholas Day	*Builder*	Fidel Nanton
DC Park	Stephen Tompkinson	*Landlord*	Arthur Whybrow
Benny McLeish	Andrew McCulloch		
Dr Hardman	Terrence Hardiman		
Donald	Roger Brierley	Producer	Ian Toynton
Receptionist	Joanna Wake	Director	Diarmuid Lawrence
Man in café	Michael Watkins	Executive Producer	John Hambley

Arthur becomes badly stressed when his doctor orders him to give up alcohol and tobacco for a few months. When Benny McLeish demands a refund on a consignment of paint and he learns of Benny's violent background, Arthur becomes convinced that his life is in danger. A stranger drinking coffee in a café and a drinker with crutches in the Winchester are both taken as major threats to his security. But he is unable to convince DS Morley that he needs police protection. Ray comes up with a plan to square things with Benny — but the police are not around when he needs them.

Episode 79

First transmission: 17 October 1991

A Bird in the Hand is Worth Two in Shepherd's Bush
by David A. Yallop

Arthur . . . . George Cole	*Club secretary* . . . . Johnny Allen
Ray . . . . Gary Webster	*Club members* . . . . Duggie Brown,
Dave . . . . Glynn Edwards	. . . . Gordon Wharmby
Billy . . . . George Costigan	*Operator* . . . . Joe Belcher
Nostalgic . . . . Nick Reding	*Nightclub manager* . . . . Bev Willis
Donna . . . . Gabrielle Cowburn	*Italian waiter* . . . Frank Rozelaar-Green
Bert Daley . . . . Sidney Livingstone		
Doreen Daley . . . . Lill Roughley	Producer . . . . Ian Toynton
Stan Sorrell . . . . Willie Ross	Director . . . . Roger Bamford
Hotel waiter . . . . Stephen Churchett	Executive Producer . . . . John Hambley

Arthur sends Ray up north to collect a valuable racing pigeon, 'Young Sam', that will be racing from London to Bradford against 'Pride of Pudsey' for a stake of £10,000. But Ray falls in love while he is in Bradford and his mind is not on his work. The pigeon goes missing and Arthur and Ray return to Bradford to try to find a replacement on the railway station. Meanwhile, Arthur is worried about Ray's new romance and calls on his contact 'Nostalgic' to bring it to an end.

Stephen Churchett, who has a small part as a hotel waiter in this episode, also wrote the stage play *Heritage* in which George Cole appeared a few years later as a proud Chelsea Pensioner. Churchett is better known now for his regular appearances as a solicitor in BBC-1's *EastEnders*.

Episode 80

Season 8/8   First transmission: 24 October 1991

Him Indoors
by Iain Roy and Chris Kelly

Arthur	George Cole	*Vagrant*	John Atkinson
Ray	Gary Webster	*Barmaid*	Joanna Bacon
Dave	Glynn Edwards	*Mr Fong*	Kim Teoh
DS Morley	Nicholas Day	*Cabbie*	Adrian McLoughlin
DC Park	Stephen Tompkinson	*Liam*	Joseph Hutton
Ron	Kenneth Colley		
Insp York	Simon Rouse		
PC Corman	Alex Lowe	Producer	Ian Toynton
PC Howard	Gareth Marks	Director	Roger Bamford
Imran	Tariq Alibai	Executive Producer	John Hambley

Arthur is trying his hand at selling security equipment. But when Rob, an ex-burglar, opens the lockup with a metal comb, he convinces Arthur to install a roller door. Unluckily for Arthur, the door jams as he is about to leave and he is forced to spend the night minding the lockup and to miss the celebration he planned for 'er indoors' birthday. During the night he is arrested by an overzealous police officer who suspects him of having broken into the lockup, and is reduced to borrowing a guard dog to give him some protection. Meanwhile, one of the properties on Arthur's security installation list is broken into and Arthur and Ray suspect that Rob the Burglar is responsible. Acting on a hunch, Ray goes to another property on the list and catches Rob red-handed. Coincidentally, the overzealous police officer acts on the same hunch and finds Ray and Rob leaving the premises. Arthur has to invent a story that sounds convincing to DS Morley. When he returns to the lockup, Arthur has to face the guard dog once again.

Highlight: Alone and bored in the lockup overnight, Arthur entertains himself doing an impersonation of Rolf Harris.

Episode 81

Season 8/9   First transmission: 31 October 1991

The Greatest Show in Willesden
by Kevin Sperring and Bernard Dempsey

Arthur	George Cole	Len	Frank Mills
Ray	Gary Webster	Vernon	Larry Barnes
Dave	Glynn Edwards	Colin Stamp	John Rutland
Tommy	John Cater	Manageress	Jenny Logan
Gloria	Emma Cunningham	Heckler	Andrew Frame
Monty	Harry Landis	Luigi Gabadini	Jimmy Lambert
Mrs Gabadini	Pauline Letts		
Barry	Steven O'Donnell		
Trevor	Mark Duffy	Producer	Ian Toynton
Diarmid	Denis Quilligan	Director	Derek Banham
Percy	James Ottaway	Executive Producer	John Hambley

Arthur installs a karaoke machine in a pub on the manor and brings in Tommy Pickford, an old stager from the music hall days, to do a ventriloquism act with his dummy 'Mystic Mickie'. The combination is a roaring success and brings in business from other pubs in the area. But Tommy falls sick and they have to audition for new talent. Then the karaoke machine is stolen from the van. Ray tries to borrow a replacement from his old school pal Barry and discovers who was behind the theft of the original one. Arthur comes up with a way to get the stolen machine back to its original owner and to get even with Barry. John Cater, still highly memorable from his role as Starr, the doorman in *The Duchess of Duke Street*, does a commendable job as Tommy Pickford the elderly ventriloquist.

Episode 82

Season 8/10   First transmission: 7 November 1991

Too Many Crooks
by Tony Jordan

Arthur . . . . George Cole	*Arnie* . . . . Godfrey James
Ray . . . . Gary Webster	*Colin* . . . . Dennis Blanch
Dave . . . . Glynn Edwards	*Police sergeant* . . . . Andy Rashleigh
DS Morley . . . . Nicholas Day	*Dennis* . . . . Andrew Dunford
DC Park . . . . Stephen Tompkinson	*Vinny's minder* . . . . David Harewood
Billy Meadows . . . . Trevor Byfield	
Vinny Meadows . . . . David Sibley	
Sadie Meadows . . . . . . Suzannah Corbett	Producer . . . . Ian Toynton
Henri . . . . David Marrick	Director . . . . Alister Hallum
Mandy . . . . Susan Watkins	Executive Producer . . . John Hambley

Vinny Meadows, a powerful villain on Arthur's patch, has a brother Billy working in the same profession in the Midlands but has not seen him for 15 years after a family dispute. Billy doesn't usually leave Birmingham as he has a phobia about travelling. When he drives down to London late one night, the police suspect that it must be for something big. No one would imagine that the object of Billy's interest is Henri, the young French chef whom Arthur has employed for his new business 'Daley Catering'. But when Vinny learns that his brother is looking for Henri he also sets out to find him to discover why Henri is so important. When Henri is finally located, his absence from a function being catered by Arthur leaves Arthur and Ray no alternative but to do the catering themselves.

Episode 83

Season 8/11   First transmission: 14 November 1991

The Odds Couple
by Tony Jordan and Liane Aukin

Arthur	George Cole	*Betty*	Delena Kidd
Ray	Gary Webster	*Receptionist*	Helen Adie
Dave	Glynn Edwards	*Alan*	Colin Higgins
Lewis Nelson	Lee Montague	*Croupiers*	Genevieve Allenbury,
Lorna Nelson	Hetty Baynes		Elaine Murray
Carlo Vincetti	Joseph Long	*Waitress*	Sally Millest
Joe	Louis Hilyer		
Eric	Neale Goodrum	Producer	Ian Toynton
Billy	Piers Ibbotson	Director	Keith Washington
Roger	Anthony May	Executive Producer	John Hambley

Lewis Nelson and Arthur have known each other for 30 years. Arthur sold Lewis his first car, which broke down on the East India Dock Road and caused a three-mile tailback. Lewis asks Arthur if he could borrow Ray for a while to look after his wife. She has a gambling problem and Lewis wants her to be kept away from the casinos. Safely away from her husband's clutches, she suggests to Arthur that he go to the casino to bet for her using her stake money. Arthur meanwhile has a sideline collecting used playing cards from the casinos and repackaging them for sale. When his messenger Eric inadvertently collects a bag of cash instead of playing cards outside a casino, Arthur believes he has made a windfall — until he discovers that the cash was stolen by Lewis to pay for his wife's debts. And Lewis wants it back.

Episode 84

　　　　　　　　First transmission: 21 November 1991

The Coach that Came In From the Cold
by Kevin Clark

Arthur	George Cole	*Major Beatty*	Patrick Godfrey
Ray	Gary Webster	*Mr Corelli*	Brian Greene
Dave	Glynn Edwards	*Mrs Corelli*	Margaret Robertson
DS Morley	Nicholas Day	*Hart*	Martin Milman
DC Park	Stephen Tompkinson	*Rambo*	Clive Kneller
Previous	Trevor Peacock		
Supt Roden	Geoffrey Whitehead		
Denny Willis	Rory Edwards	Producer	Ian Toynton
Lorraine	Lisa Jacobs	Director	Richard Standeven
Simon Perkins	Simon Cowell-Parker	Executive Producer	John Hambley

Under pressure to produce a favourable annual audit, Morley's superintendent sells Arthur a police coach that is surplus to requirements. Arthur
immediately sees the potential to provide a sightseeing service for tourists.
But Arthur has to provide an impromptu commentary in response to the
tourists' demands; the tourists have to push the coach when it breaks down,
and when Arthur takes the tourists into the Winchester Club for a drink they
witness the spectacle of him being threatened by a group of heavies. Arthur
has other concerns when he tries to become a full member of a local golf
club. His attempts are thwarted by his acquaintance with 'Previous' who was
recently released from the Scrubs and is now a caddy at the club. Ray, however,
discovers from one of the club's staff that the new captain of the club has
engineered a scheme to sell the club to make way for executive apartments
within the next six months and will benefit personally from the sale. When
Arthur claims that he is responsible for the discovery, his membership seems
assured. Jokes about handicaps and having rounds abound. Arthur's quick
thinking gets the superintendent off the hook. 'Previous' produces an English
conversation tape for foreign tourists.

　　Stephen Tompkinson is credited as DC Park but does not actually appear
in the episode.

Episode 85

Season 8/13

First transmission: 25 December 1991

The Cruel Canal

by Kevin Sperring and Bernard Dempsey

Arthur . . . . George Cole	*Freddie* . . . . Michael Goldie
Ray . . . . Gary Webster	*Canal policeman* . . . . .Metin Marlow
Dave . . . . Glynn Edwards	*Traffic policeman* . . . . Richard Heap
Big Dai . . . . .Anthony O'Donnell	
Gloria . . . . .Emma Cunningham	
Two-Tone . . . . .Neil Phillips	Producer . . . . .Ian Toynton
Vicky . . . . Cathy Murphy	Director . . . . .Keith Washington
Derek . . . . Trevor Cooper	Executive Producer . . . .John Hambley

Arthur buys a van load of video players of questionable origin, hoping to sell them to 'Two-Tone', a major fence for electronic equipment in Limehouse. But 'Two-Tone' temporarily cancels the order when Ray's van breaks down in heavy traffic and he is unable to deliver them on time. With no space to store the video players at the lockup, Arthur leaves them at the Winchester. However, the arrival of the diminutive but vicious Big Dai at the Winchester, bemoaning the fact that he has had some videos stolen, warns Arthur that he has to get the videos away from the club and delivered to Limehouse as soon as possible. With no van and the roads jammed, Arthur hits on the idea of delivering them by barge through London's canal system. The journey takes longer than expected, and Arthur and Ray find themselves staying on the barge overnight, entertaining themselves playing Monopoly. The stress of the journey and their poor boating skills eventually take their toll and cause major arguments. When they finally reach Limehouse with the videos, Big Dai and 'Two-Tone' are already there on the canal bank. . . .

Episode 86

Season 9/1   First transmission: 7 January 1993

I'll Never Forget Whats 'Ername
by William Ivory

Arthur	George Cole	Anderson	Simon Kunz
Ray	Gary Webster	Trevor	David Hounslow
Dave	Glynn Edwards	Building society cashier	Sukie Smith
DS Morley	Nicholas Day	Cabbie	Tony Collins
DC Field	Jonty Stephens	Cinema cashier	Joanna Brookes
Walter	Kenneth Cranham	Car lot man	Dave Atkins
Marty	Allan Corduner	Librarian	Diana Payan
Bert	Sidney Livingstone	Baths attendant	John Barrard
Doreen	Lill Roughley		
Quiz master	David Howey	Producer	Ian Toynton
Governor	Mark Brignal	Director	Lawrence Gordon Clark
Fast Eddie	Bill Moody	Executive Producer	John Hambley

Dave inadvertently enters a team from the Winchester Club for a Quiz Night organised by a brewery. Arthur is initially reluctant to take part — until he discovers that his old rival Walter is leading the opposition. But with only Arthur, Ray and Dave on the team, they need one more person. The unexpected arrival of Arthur's old business partner, Marty 'Brains' Goldblum, at the lockup makes him the obvious choice. The fact that Marty has just escaped from an open prison does not deter Arthur, who arranges temporary refuge for him at Bert and Doreen's place. Morley, meanwhile, who has a personal score to settle with Marty, suspects that Arthur knows more than he admits about Marty's whereabouts. After being pursued by Morley and Field in a sauna, and unable to continue his masquerade to Bert and Doreen as a non-English speaker, Marty decides to give himself up. It seems that there will be an incomplete team for the quiz — until Ray finds help from an unexpected quarter.

Episode 87

Season 9/2   First transmission: 14 January 1993

No Way to Treat a Daley
by Tim Firth

Arthur	George Cole	*Kenny*	Hugh Sachs
Ray	Gary Webster	*Mr Ali*	Nabil Massad
Dave	Glynn Edwards	*Waiter*	Nadio Fortune
Warren	Richard Ridings	*Pump attendant*	Matthew Lloyd-Lewis
Gloria	Emma Cunningham	*Gas delivery man*	Nick Raggett
Pike	Philip Martin Brown		
Les	Desmond McNamara	Producer	Ian Toynton
Joey	James Berwick	Director	Lawrence Gordon Clark
Desiree	Suzy Cooper	Executive Producer	John Hambley

Arthur discovers an aerial advertising balloon amongst some fire-damaged stock and recognises the potential of the advertising business. But Warren, the minder of someone who is already in the business, sees Ray while he is inflating the balloon at a petrol station and reports the matter to his boss. When his boss, Tony Pike, hears about the possible competition he sends Warren to bring Arthur to him for a chat. Warren takes Arthur to a disused industrial building in the marshes to wait for Pike. While they are waiting, Arthur manages to establish a rapport with Warren and engages him in a sensitive dialogue in which Warren reveals his hatred for Pike and of the type of work Pike forces him to do. Ray, meanwhile, tries frantically to locate Arthur and is introduced to Les, who suffered at the hands of Pike previously and is now badly crippled as a result. Ray persuades Les to help him locate the building where Arthur is being held. When Ray arrives, Arthur is not to be found, but Ray manages to teach Pike a lesson. Dejected, Ray returns to the lockup and finds Arthur, pleased to have set Warren's life straight through his words of wisdom and a changed man himself as a result.

Subplots: Ray's girlfriend Gloria photographs the balloon and gets stood up while Ray is searching for Arthur. Ray causes a fight at a boxing match.

Episode 88

Season 9/3 First transmission: 21 January 1993

Uneasy Rider
by Geoff Rowley

Arthur	George Cole	Susie	Sara Stewart
Ray	Gary Webster	Jehovah's Witnesses	Jeff Rawle,
Dave	Glynn Edwards		Christopher Ettridge
DS Morley	Nicholas Day	Big Malc	Richard Brenner
DC Field	Jonty Stephens	Marks	Roger Martin
Conway	Ben Chaplin	Laura Kaye	Annie Lambert
Ralphy	Ian Bartholomew		
Keef	Nick Dunning	Producer	Ian Toynton
Rabbit	Brian Hibbard	Director	Diarmuid Lawrence
Trish	Elaine Lordan	Executive Producer	John Hambley

When Arthur acquires an old-fashioned minicab console he decides to set up a document courier business from the lockup under the name of 'The Daley Post'. He recruits Rabbit, a biker with a phenomenal knowledge of London streets and landmarks, to help him. When Ralphy and Keef, the proprietors of a competing courier business, pay Arthur a call and offer him some of their dissatisfied customers to start him off, Arthur is grateful for the gesture. But when the customers turn out to be empty offices, and the packages contain stolen property, forged driving licences and fake sports fixture tickets, Arthur realises that he has been set up. And when packages start to go missing and Arthur is terrorised by a customer looking for a portfolio of nude photographs, Arthur decides to close the business at short notice. Meanwhile, Ray comes up with a plan to get even with Ralphy and Keef.

Subplot: Arthur is selling London street name plaques to Gunter, his contact in Germany. Arthur becomes unusually interested when a pair of Jehovah's Witnesses visits him.

Episode 89

Season 9/4 First transmission: 28 January 1993

Looking for Mr. Goodtime
by David A. Yallop

Arthur	George Cole	*Miss Brown*	Eileen Bell
Ray	Gary Webster	*John*	Colin Spaull
Dave	Glynn Edwards	*Desk sergeant*	David Hobbs
DS Morley	Nicholas Day	*Female guest*	Julia Goodman
DC Field	Jonty Stephens	*Male guests*	Jeffrey Robert, Alan Palmer
Tomkins	Jim Carter	*Billy Mortimer*	Barny Clevely
Lockwood	Colin Jeavons	*Jailer*	Russell Milton
Ashley	Peter Baylis	*Inspector*	David Brocklehurst
DC Reed	Ian Keith	*Bailiff*	Paul Kelly
Mel Taylor	Ronnie Letham		
Stuart	Rene Zagger		
Syd	Philip Manikum		
Prosecuting counsel	Amanda Burton		
Magistrate	Alan Rowe	Producer	Ian Toynton
Willie	David KS Tse	Director	Gordon Flemyng
Tony	David Belcher	Executive Producer	John Hambley

During the annual dinner of the West London Motor Traders' Association, Arthur hears about a Daimler for sale at a knockdown price and he wants to be first in line. But first he has to track down the elusive Tony Goodtime of Goodtime Motors who is selling the car. Arthur's attempts to locate the company eventually lead to his arrest for propositioning a woman in the street and assaulting a police officer. This time, even Sergeant Morley doubts his guilt, but Ray has seen Arthur behaving very strangely recently and has his suspicions. Things do not look good for Arthur as he defends himself in court — until Ray tracks down Mr Goodtime and a surprise witness.

Subplot: Arthur is selling red light bulbs to a Chinese restaurant.

Episode 90

Season 9/5   First transmission: 4 February 1993

Opportunity Knocks and Bruises
by Chris Kelly and Iain Roy

Arthur	George Cole	Cecil	Chris Matthews
Ray	Gary Webster	Wigmore	Freddie Stuart
Dave	Glynn Edwards	Bank teller	Orla Brady
DS Morley	Nicholas Day	Secretary	Melee Hutton
DC Field	Jonty Stephens	Lad	Francis Pope
Alexie Nolan	Sean McGinley		
Amanda	Natalie Roles		
Mrs Mitchell	Eliza Buckingham	Producer	Ian Toynton
Cllr Griffiths	Robert Blythe	Director	Diarmuid Lawrence
Mr Fairchild	Brian McGrath	Executive Producer	John Hambley

Arthur does a deal with Alexie Nolan, a fairground manager, who agrees to take some of Arthur's surplus stock as fairground prizes. But Nolan manages to outsmart Arthur by trading him a fruit machine for the stock instead of paying cash. Realising his mistake, Arthur selects a fruit machine that Nolan definitely did not intend to trade. When he installs it in the Winchester he finds himself in danger of being arrested for not having a gaming licence and, worse still, for fraud. Ray finds a way to deliver the real culprit to Morley.

Subplots: Ray has difficulty managing his time while his new girlfriend Amanda is working as a nurse on night duty. Arthur is supplying astronomical telescopes for security purposes for the Neighbourhood Watch Committee ('you can spot nefarious characters on Venus, never mind the end of the road').

Episode 91

First transmission: 11 February 1993

Gone With the Winchester
by Bernard Dempsey and Kevin Sperring

Arthur . . . . George Cole	*Dermot* . . . . Peter Gowen
Ray . . . . Gary Webster	*Winchester regulars* . . . . Terry John,
Dave . . . . Glynn Edwards	. . . . Aaron Harris, Terry Mortimer
Toby Jug Johnson . . . . James Booth	*Carlos* . . . . Romolo Bruni
Bert . . . . Sidney Livingstone	
Doreen . . . . Lill Roughley	
Gloria . . . . Emma Cunningham	Producer . . . . Ian Toynton
Jimmy the Jeweller . . . . John Levitt	Director . . . . . Lawrence Gordon Clark
Len . . . . Frank Mills	Executive Producer . . . . John Hambley

This episode sees a reappearance of James Booth who first appeared in Episode 59 in September 1985 as an old lag who was fond of using the expression 'blah, blah, blah — b'boom'. This episode casts him as Toby Jug Johnson, a member of Arthur and Dave's boyhood gang (the Brentford Backhanders).

When Toby is released from prison after a lengthy sentence he meets up with his old pals at the Winchester Club and they begin reminiscing about their boyhood days. As the stories are retold, Arthur begins to suspect that Dave has been double-crossing him over the years. When Arthur sees Dave finalising a secret deal with Jimmy the Jeweller, another member of the old gang, he thinks that Dave is transferring Arthur's share in the Winchester Club to Jimmy. Arthur retaliates by setting up a rival bar to the Winchester but discovers that the staff he has put together for the project are sadly lacking in experience. He also discovers that good friendships last and that thieves can't be trusted.

Episode 92

Season 9/7   First transmission: 18 February 1993

How to Succeed in Business Without Really Retiring
by William Ivory

Arthur	George Cole	*Lenny*	Gordon Winter
Ray	Gary Webster	*Colin*	Mark McKenna
Dave	Glynn Edwards	*Flash*	Geoffrey Larder
Bert	Sidney Livingstone	*Norman*	John Halstead
Hapless	John Normington	*Young boy*	Max Murray Burrows
Delilah	Liz Fraser	*DS Harris*	Philip Childs
Janice	Helen Masters	*Monty*	Robert Demeger
Alf	Colin Farrell		
Bechers	Lewis George		
Harold	Nigel Gregory	Producer	Ian Toynton
Stella	Debbi Blythe	Director	Richard Standeven
Pete	Andrew Bailey	Executive Producer	John Hambley

Arthur decides to retire and leave Ray in charge of the business after he hears
great things from Hapless Harry about retirement. But retirement doesn't
agree with him and he finds himself with too much time on his hands.
Meanwhile, despite Ray's good work in computerising the business, he still
has a lot to learn. When Ray falls victim to a sting operation involving stolen
jewellery, Arthur tracks down the perpetrators using his contacts and years
of experience and sets up his own sting to teach them a lesson.

Episode 93

Season 9/8

First transmission: 25 February 1993

The Roof of All Evil
by William Ivory

Arthur	George Cole	*Steve*	Kevin Dignam
Ray	Gary Webster	*House owner*	Simon Molloy
Dave	Glynn Edwards		
Logie	Pete Postlethwaite	Producer	Ian Toynton
Fingers Rossetti	Philip Locke	Director	Gordon Flemyng
Isabella	Liza Walker	Executive Producer	John Hambley

Arthur sees great potential in satellite dishes for home television reception. He buys a consignment from Germany but is unable to assemble them because the instructions are in German. He therefore calls on his old pal Logie, an electronics wizard, to help with the assembly and installation. When Ray takes an order for a satellite dish from Fingers Rossetti, Arthur becomes very anxious to cancel it as Rossetti has a reputation for taking vicious revenge whenever he is crossed (hence his nickname 'Fingers', as these often end up missing). Arthur and Ray visit Rossetti but he has no intention of cancelling the deal because he has invited some friends over to watch a soccer match on the satellite channel. But as a goodwill gesture to Arthur he invites him clay pigeon shooting. Ray meanwhile discovers that Rossetti has banned his daughter Isabella, an old schoolmate of Ray's, from seeing Steve whom she intends to marry. Ray sets out to resolve this problem and leaves Arthur and Logie to install the dish, unaware that Logie is scared of heights. Arthur tries to give Logie some support but they both become stranded on the roof.

Episode 94

First transmission: 4 March 1993

Last Orders at the Winchester
by Gary Lawson and John Phelps

Arthur	George Cole	Arnie	Frankie Cosgrave
Ray	Gary Webster	DS Thorp	Julian Gartside
Dave	Glynn Edwards	Harry	James Saxon
DS Morley	Nicholas Day	Sandra	Michele Winstanley
DC Field	Jonty Stephens	Vicar	Basil Moss
'Heart Attack'	Geoffrey Hutchings	Surveyor	Dan Strauss
Vic	Gavin Richards	Receptionist	Anna Mackmin
Gloria	Emma Cunningham	Singer	Alice McDonald
Barry	Aaron Harris		
George	Barry McCarthy	Producer	Ian Toynton
Little Pete	George Sweeney	Director	AJ Quinn
Monty	George Raistrick	Executive Producer	John Hambley

Arthur arranges to redecorate the Winchester Club to celebrate Dave's 25-year association with the club. But the plans go badly wrong when 'Heart Attack' (to whom Arthur has entrusted the work) removes a load-bearing wall and causes £35,000 of damage and closure of the club. A new pub opened by Vic following his reappearance on the manor provides an alternative place for the Winchester regulars to drink, but Vic's reappearance coincides with an increase in the number of arrests in the area. Meanwhile, a charity auction and football match fielding the Winchester regulars against the police is arranged to raise funds for the Winchester's repair. To show his remorse at the damage he caused, 'Heart Attack' temporarily revisits his previous profession as a burglar to help raise funds. The auction provides a way to make the funds appear legitimate. But Vic discovers that nobody loves a grass.

Episode 95

Season 9/10   First transmission: 11 March 1993

Cars and Pints and Pains
by David A. Yallop

Arthur	George Cole	*Phil*	Chris Sanders
Ray	Gary Webster	*Taxi driver*	Alan Talbot
Dave	Glynn Edwards	*Car thief*	John Quarmby
DS Morley	Nicholas Day	*Policewoman*	Rita Gerza
DC Field	Jonty Stephens	*1st policeman*	Paul Trussell
Winston	Dhobi Oparei	*2nd policeman*	Ian Minney
Linda	Juliette Grassby		
Sarah	Rebecca Lamb		
Dean Cooper	David Boyce	Producer	Ian Toynton
Jarvis	Chris Hunter	Director	Lawrence Gordon Clark
Tony	Andy Lucas	Executive Producer	John Hambley

Times are getting tough in the motor trade. Arthur hasn't sold a used car for more than three weeks. Dave is having similar trouble getting customers into the Winchester Club. Since he can't sell his cars, Arthur hits on the idea of renting them out. To make the deal even more attractive, he includes a free space at a car boot sale and an invitation to a half-price happy hour at the Winchester Club with each rental. Ray recruits the services of his friend Winston to help on the project but, in his enthusiasm, Winston rents out Arthur's Daimler. Morley, meanwhile, has enough on his plate with a spate of housebreakings and jewellery thefts in the district. But with the opening of Arthur's new business, he finds himself even more concerned with an outbreak of stolen cars being driven around the manor. Arthur has to come to terms not only with the loss of his Daimler but also the indignity of being locked out by 'er indoors.

Episode 96

Season 9/10   First transmission: 18 March 1993

The Great Trilby
by Bernard Dempsey and Kevin Sperring

Arthur	George Cole	Timmons	Michael Vaughan
Ray	Gary Webster	Mabel	Margery Withers
Dave	Glynn Edwards	Teller	Richard Platt
DS Morley	Nicholas Day	Supervisor	Ian Barritt
DC Field	Jonty Stephens	Receptionist	Adlyn Ross
Bill McCabe	Simon Chilvers	Secretary	Sarah Carpenter
Muldier	Pip Torrens	Ethel	Pat Rossiter
Gloria	Emma Cunningham		
Spiky	Frank Baker		
Dayglow	Richard Avery	Producer	Ian Toynton
Nobby Green	Simon Holmes	Director	Roger Bamford
Vicar	Thomas Wheatley	Executive Producer	John Hambley

This is the first part of a trilogy involving Arthur and Ray's visit to Sydney to prove Arthur's claim to an inheritance.

Things are going bad for Arthur. He can't get credit, his car is towed away, and his cash card is swallowed up by the automatic teller machine. But things begin to look more rosy when McCabe, a private investigator, appears at the Winchester Club searching for Arthur to tell him that he may be the heir to the estate of a distant relative who has died in Australia. Arthur first has to provide documentary evidence that he is the rightful heir. With partial details obtained from the Public Records Office and a genealogist, Arthur and Ray find the evidence they need from the headstone of a grave. Arthur is presented with two business class tickets to Sydney and suddenly becomes everyone's friend. In the meantime, he has been displaying fake parking tickets on his car to avoid paying parking fees. When Morley arrests him it seems that the inheritance will be lost, as a criminal record will make him ineligible.

Ray does a favour for DC Field and Field returns the favour.

Episode 97

Season 9/11 First transmission: 25 March 1993

A Taste of Money
by William Ivory

Arthur	George Cole	*Johnson*	Kerry Blakeman
Ray	Gary Webster	*Ross*	Boris Brkic
Bill McCabe	Simon Chilvers	*Evans' secretary*	Diana Cole
Reid	Bill Hunter		
Susan Hamilton	Nikki Coghill		
Rod Thompson	Alex Morcos	Producer	Ian Toynton
Geoffrey Evans	Arthur Dignam	Director	Roger Bamford
Concierge	Robert Alexander	Executive Producer	John Hambley

This episode is the second of the trilogy concerning the estate of Arthur's deceased great uncle Joshua. The episode is jointly produced by Euston Films and the Australian Broadcasting Corporation and has two associate producers credited: one for the UK and one for Australia.

Arthur and Ray are invited to Sydney, Australia by the executor of the late Joshua Daley's estate to establish Arthur's claim that he is the rightful beneficiary. Arthur has trouble adjusting to the demands of contemporary air travel. On his arrival in Sydney he is horrified to learn that Bill McCabe, a private investigator, has tracked down several other possible claimants. Ray drives Arthur to visit the estate, known as Paradise Springs, but the car breaks down in the desert and they become stranded.

Episode 98

First transmission: 1 April 1993

For a Few Dollars More
by Bernard Dempsey and Kevin Sperring

Arthur	George Cole	Men in pub	Rob Hunter, John Meillon Jr
Ray	Gary Webster	Burger stall owner	Nic Gazzana
Reid	Bill Hunter	Receptionist	Hugh Wade
Collins	Terry Gill	Deidre	Cate Murray
Robyn	Danielle Spencer	Policeman	Michael Burgess
Concierge	Robert Alexander	Bellboy	Troy Rowley
Davis	Roy Billing		
Swan	Mark Strickson		
Manager	George Leppard	Producer	Ian Toynton
Ross	Boris Brkic	Director	Roger Bamford
Mary Maguire	Carole Skinner	Executive Producer	John Hambley

This is the conclusion of the trilogy concerning the estate of Arthur's deceased great uncle Joshua. The opening credit sequence is a cleverly arranged adaptation of the usual closing sequence and sees Arthur and Ray walking across Sydney Harbour Bridge. As they are walking, Arthur realises that he has left something behind. They hesitate for a while but, unlike the original sequence, decide to continue on their way.

Unaware that he has been tricked out of his inheritance, Arthur is stranded in Sydney with no money, no air ticket, and a huge hotel bill. Arthur and Ray have no alternative but to find employment. Ray does his bit at a burger stall and in a pub, while Arthur manages to find work doing what he does best: selling on the street. But when he tries selling to the wrong person, Arthur finds himself in trouble with the police and with the people who cheated him. He is given 24 hours to leave Australia.

This episode is another joint production of Euston Films and the Australian Broadcasting Corporation.

Episode 99

Season 10/1 First transmission: 6 January 1994

A Fridge Too Far
by Bernard Dempsey and Kevin Sperring ·

Arthur	George Cole	*Mr Gordon*	Christopher Owen
Ray	Gary Webster	*Mrs Kravitz*	Dilys Watling
Dave	Glynn Edwards	*Fire chief*	Chris Driscoll
Mervyn Kravitz	Linal Haft	*Bingo ticket girl*	Iona Kennedy
Lucy Conti	Lesley Duff	*Queen*	Nick Gillard
Gino	Paul Reynolds	*Madonna*	Colin Wyatt
Marty	Che Walker		
Tewkesbury	Tony Steedman	Producer	Ian Toynton
Wayne	Shaun Dingwall	Director	Charles Beeson
Brian	Jim McManus	Executive Producer	John Hambley

Arthur cannot pass up the chance to buy a batch of fridge-freezers at a knockdown price. To pay for them he uses the funds he intended to use for a stock of mopeds he hopes to supply to the pizza man. But to raise the original cash he pawned 'er indoors' jewellery. When one of the freezers blows up and badly damages the house of Mervyn, the moped supplier, Mervyn keeps Arthur's money as compensation instead of delivering the mopeds. Arthur therefore comes up with a scheme to fake a robbery at the lockup and claim the insurance payment. The robbery, to be conducted by two of Ray's pals, goes badly wrong when a genuine robbery takes place seconds before the fake one. Ray realises that there must have been a tip-off and has a good idea where it came from. Arthur then discovers that Mervyn is having an extramarital relationship and uses this as a lever to recover the mopeds he is owed. He also finds a way to see the end of the faulty freezers. But what about 'er indoors' jewellery?

Episode 100

Season 10/2   First transmission: 13 January 1994

Another Case of Van Blank
by William Ivory

Arthur	George Cole	*Customs officer*	Stephen Oxley
Ray	Gary Webster	*Matelot*	Nicholas Mead
Dave	Glynn Edwards		
Madeleine	Mylene Demongeot		
Henry	David Simeon		
Rochelle	Olivier Pierre	Producer	Ian Toynton
Wally	Peter Cleall	Director	Ken Hannam
Passport officer	John Leeson	Executive Producer	John Hambley

Arthur, Ray and Dave take a trip to France to benefit from relaxed restrictions on the importation of liquor. But Arthur's contact Henry proves unreliable and they are forced to stay overnight at a cheap hotel awaiting delivery of the consignment the following day. Ray and Dave try to make the trip worthwhile by buying alcohol at the hypermarket, but the theft of their purchases overnight from their van leads them to the police station — where Arthur does not endear himself to the local police chief. The following day Arthur meets up again with Henry and goes out with him to collect the goods, little knowing that they are about to be stolen from a warehouse. The arrival of the police during the theft sees Arthur back at the police station, this time under arrest for being an accomplice. His prospects do not look good.

Peter Cleall, who played Duffy in the 1960s comedy series *Please Sir*, appears as Wally, who first introduces the idea of importing cheap liquor to Arthur.

Episode 101

Season 10/3   First transmission: 20 January 1994

All Things Brighton Beautiful
by Tony Hoare

Arthur	George Cole	*Betty*	Diana Berriman
Ray	Gary Webster	*Woman in Brighton*	Susan Derrick
Dave	Glynn Edwards	*Traffic cop*	Roderick Nicolson
Sidney	Andrew Sachs	*Receptionist*	Stephen Reynolds
Bernie	Peter Kelly		
Sadie	Sheila Steafel	Producer	Ian Toynton
Skinhead	Liam McKenna	Director	Gordon Flemyng
Skinhead's mate	Daniel Earl	Executive Producer	John Hambley

An old friend of Arthur's, Sidney Myers (played by Andrew Sachs from *Fawlty Towers*), has himself delivered to the lockup in a crate and explains that he was recently diagnosed with a terminal illness. Unable to face the prospect of living through the illness he paid £500 to a skinhead he met in a pub to kill him during the next two weeks. Only after making the arrangements did he learn that the doctor had made a mistake and he was not dying after all. He explains that he went to Arthur for protection for two weeks until the contract had expired. Coincidentally, Arthur has been asked by Dave's sister to sell her late husband's caravan. Arthur seizes the opportunity to secrete Sidney away in the caravan in a field by the racetrack in Brighton. The plans go awry, however, and the caravan rolls down a slope and bursts into flames, leaving Arthur and Sidney to rough it overnight. Meanwhile, back in London, Ray traces the skinhead and learns about a vicious psychopath, Bernie the Bosh, who has just been released from prison and is very anxious to track down Sidney.

This is listed in the *TV Times* as the 100th episode of *Minder* (the Christmas special in 1983 made up of excerpts from a number of previous episodes was not included in the total). This episode dispenses with the usual opening and closing sequences. The opening credits are played over footage of the packing case being delivered to the lockup, and the closing sequence plays the credits over footage of Arthur in the congregation of a Salvation Army hostel singing *Onward Christian Soldiers* to the accompaniment of a full brass band.

Episode 102

First transmission: 27 January 1994

One Flew Over the Parents' Nest
by Tony Hoare

Arthur	George Cole	*2nd heavy*	Derren Litten
Ray	Gary Webster	*Cronin*	Bernard Kay
Dave	Glynn Edwards	*Melissa*	Portia Booroff
Susie	Susannah Doyle	*Wasp*	Jake Wood
Bert	Sidney Livingstone	*Aldridge*	Martyn Whitby
Doreen	Lill Roughley	*Robert*	Andrew Hilton
Fowler	Duncan Bell		
Grey	Barry Aird		
Willie	Tony Robinson	Producer	Ian Toynton
DI Styles	John Bowler	Director	John Reardon
1st heavy	David Bauckham	Executive Producer	John Hambley

After dropping his parents at the airport at the start of their vacation, Ray does a favour for Susie, a young girl he meets at the airport, and drives her to West London. She tells Ray that she is being pursued by her abusive ex-husband and is planning to stay with a friend until she can work things out. When they reach the address, they discover that her friend has moved away without leaving a forwarding address. Arthur, sensing a nice little earner, and against Ray's better judgement, offers her the use of Ray's parents' house while they are away on vacation. Unknown to Ray and Arthur, Susie is actually being pursued by a pair of heavies and a senior police officer from Manchester. Susie, meanwhile, has other activities to take care of at the house and, as a result, Arthur is arrested for running a brothel. Ray's mother is not prepared for what she finds when she and her husband return home early from their holiday.

Subplot: Arthur employs Willie (hilariously portrayed by Tony Robinson of Baldrick fame in *The Black Adder*) to help with his dubious business selling blocks of wood by mail order. Willie has difficulty adhering to Arthur's interpretation of the Industrial Relations Act.

Episode 103

Season 10/5   First transmission: 3 February 1994

The Immaculate Contraption
by William Ivory

Arthur .... George Cole	*Priest* .... Niall Toibin
Ray .... Gary Webster	*Freddy* .... Andy Greenhalgh
Dave .... Glynn Edwards	*Jorgensen* .... Jerry Harte
Bjorn .... Metin Yenal	*Fidel* .... Joseph Alessi
Bert .... Sidney Livingstone	*Tiny* .... Perry Benson
Sister Angelica .... Frances Cuka	*Clive* .... Peter Gunn
Smiler .... Tim Wylton	*Eric* .... Morgan Jones
Dr Jarvis .... Richard Durden	*Mechanic* .... Andy Mulligan
Sister Virginia .... Edda Sharpe		
Hacksaw Harry .... Peter Shorey	Producer .... Ian Toynton
Chico .... Kevork Malikyan	Director .... Gordon Flemyng
Dipso Pete .... Mike Savage	Executive Producer .... John Hambley

Arthur's attempts to equip Dr Jorgensen's relaxation clinic go hopelessly awry after he sells a used car to a nun at a highly inflated price. The 'aqua massagers' (jacuzzis) are nowhere to be found, the exercise bikes he ordered turn out to be regular bicycles, and Arthur has to call on the assistance of an undertaker to supply the relaxation tables. His car is clamped and he is locked out of his car lot. Worse still, the menacing Chico is pressing Arthur for a consignment of video players that have become lost in transit. Could it be divine retribution? Arthur assigns Ray to repair the nun's car but feels the need to take confession to ensure that he has been completely absolved.

Episode 104
Season 10/6   First transmission: 10 February 1994
All Quiet on the West End Front
by Bernard Dempsey and Kevin Sperring

Arthur	George Cole	*Tout*	Tony Westrope
Ray	Gary Webster	*Demoman*	Gary Fairhall
Dave :	Glynn Edwards	*Gerry*	Colin Campbell
Hargreaves	Ian McNeice	*Robinson*	Nick Lucas
Marian	Samantha Janus	*Hostess*	Luzita Pope
Vanessa	Natascha Taylor	*The Actor*	David Cunningham
Kenton	Derrick Branche		
Mr Hussein	Mark Zuber	Producer	Ian Toynton
Wasp	Jake Wood	Director	Diarmuid Lawrence
Shifty	Tim Stern	Executive Producer	John Hambley

Inspired by a promoter at a business exhibition, Arthur sets up his own entertainment business 'Willesden Entertainments'. He aims to meet and greet visiting business people and provide them with dinner and after-dinner entertainment. His first attempt is a disaster and his party is far from satisfied with the dinner and the seats that he bought from a tout for *Les Misérables*. His second outing is more successful when he takes his clients to a jazz club at which Ray's girlfriend is singing. A chance meeting with the event organiser of his business exhibition gives Arthur an introduction to a plush casino at which his party appears well satisfied. We see Ray take what is probably his worst beating as a minder.

Subplot: Arthur is selling waxwork dummies of famous people and becomes interested in cinematic memorabilia in the 'art gecko' style.

Episode 105

Season 10/7 First transmission: 17 February 1994

The Great Depression of 1994
by Arthur Ellis

Arthur	George Cole	*Mrs Kean*	Merelina Kendall
Ray	Gary Webster	*Bernie*	James Coyle
Dave	Glynn Edwards	*Cecil*	Geoffrey Drew
Percy	Robert Stephens	*Joy*	Daphne Neville
Brian	Barry Jackson	*Security man*	Russell Kilmister
Henry	Peter Jones		
Heather	Amelda Brown	Producer	Ian Toynton
DS Rogerson	James Warrior	Director	Gordon Flemyng
Fowler	Duncan Bell	Executive Producer	John Hambley

Everything seems to go wrong for Arthur and the people around him when Ray's Uncle Brian suddenly develops severe depression. Arthur seeks the help of Percy, a manic depressive patient who recovered and built up a successful business selling mail order wigs. Suspecting that Brian might follow in Percy's footsteps when he recovers, Arthur prepares him for a career in the mail order wig business. Percy, however, advises Arthur to ensure that the depression is genuine and is not being faked to hide a different problem. Arthur, meanwhile, sells a car to a punter, unaware that the punter is a retired police officer who arrested him 25 years ago. When the punter comes back to the Winchester on a nostalgia trip, Arthur finds himself using the counselling skills he developed to help Brian.

Episode 106

Season 10/8   First transmission: 24 February 1994

On the Autofront
by William Ivory

Arthur	George Cole	Parker	Stuart Laing
Ray	Gary Webster	DC Lang	William Armstrong
Dave	Glynn Edwards	Darren	Peter Waddington
Tomkins	Jim Carter	Man in car lot	Sam Davis
Don Gedley	Godfrey Jackman	Lads	Demetri Jagger, Norman Roberts
Grant	Perry Fenwick		
Mike	Valentine Nonyela		
Cool K	Neville Watson	Producer	Ian Toynton
Carson	Ian Thompson	Director	Baz Taylor
Lady in garage	Soo Drouet	Executive Producer	John Hambley

Arthur is forced to cut the prices of the cars on his lot when a rival car dealer sets up business nearby. He decides to advertise on the radio to bring in customers but can only afford to use amateur disc jockeys on a pirate radio station. He realises the rivalry is serious when a punter takes a car on a test drive through the window of an antique shop and the shop owner identifies Arthur as the driver. When he and Ray track down the real driver to the rival car business, the driver's father proposes a deal in which Arthur will accept the police charges in exchange for generous compensation. But when all the windscreens on Arthur's car lot are found smashed he realises that it is time for the deal to be cancelled.

Episode 107

Season 10/9   First transmission: 3 March 1994

Bring Me the Head of Arthur Daley
by Bernard Dempsey and Kevin Sperring

Arthur . . . . George Cole	Lionel . . . . Tim Potter
Ray . . . . Gary Webster	Atkinson . . . . Patrick Pasi
Dave . . . . Glynn Edwards	Willy . . . . .Tat Whalley
Knowles . . . . Stratford Johns	Dean . . . . Sean Harris
Phelan . . . . .Kenneth Cope	Cabbie . . . . Jonathan Stratt
DS Rogerson . . . . James Warrior	Policeman . . . . .Gilly Gilchrist
Magistrate . . . . .Phyllida Law	Fitzgibbon . . . . Stephen Tate
Hammer . . . . .Jack Watson	Prison officers . . . . . .Douglas McFerran,
Bennett . . . . Alan Ford	. . . . Sebastian Abineri
Potter . . . . David Battley	
Gossip . . . . Desmond McNamara	
Rawle . . . . .Tyler Butterworth	
Harding . . . . David Cardy	
Rossitor . . . . .Jeff Nuttall	Producer . . . . .Ian Toynton
Doctor . . . . Tim Munro	Director . . . . .John Stroud
Armitage . . . . Richard Braine	Executive Producer . . . .John Hambley

Arthur's car has a minor scrape with a taxi and before long he finds himself charged with a hit and run offence in which several parked cars were reported to have been damaged by his car. Later he is sentenced to 100 hours of community service for handling stolen property after selling a carpet he discovers at the lockup. When Ray finds an attaché case full of expensive wristwatches at the lockup just before the police arrive it becomes clear that someone is setting Arthur up, but who and why? Their enquiries lead them to Knowles, who is serving a life sentence for his part in a sorting office robbery. Arthur discovers that he sold the car used in the getaway to Knowles and that the gang was arrested because the car broke down during the getaway. Knowles holds Arthur responsible and now wants to take revenge on him. But Arthur discovers evidence that should stop any more attempts to set him up.

Episode 108

Season 10/10   First transmission: 10 March 1994

The Long Good Thursday
by Tony Hoare

Arthur	George Cole	*Rosie*	Jean Warren
Ray	Gary Webster	*Phil*	Matthew Delamere
Dave	Glynn Edwards	*Billy*	John Bardon
Frankie	Matthew Scurfield	*Newscaster*	Trevor Nichols
Luigi	Chris Sanders		
Carla	Mary Maddox	Producer	Ian Toynton
Sammon	Neil McCaul	Director	Lawrence Gordon Clark
Riley	Barnaby Kay	Executive Producer	John Hambley

Arthur's plans to open an Italian-Greek restaurant (the 'Casa Noshtra') with Luigi are upset when Frankie Connor appears at the lockup brandishing a gun shortly after his escape from prison. Frankie once did some casual work for Arthur and believes that Arthur may be able to help him identify the person who has been having an affair with his wife while he was in prison. Inside, he earned the nickname 'Cranky Frankie' because of his vicious behaviour. Now, in a highly disturbed state of mind, he demands that Arthur arrange for Frankie's wife to be brought to the lockup so that he can confront her about the affair. He threatens Arthur with serious harm if he is not able to arrange the meeting with his wife or informs the police. But then Frankie discovers that Arthur's business partner Luigi is the man involved in the affair and demands to go to the Winchester Club to meet him. Once there, he holds Arthur, Ray and Dave hostage while waiting for Luigi to arrive, unaware that Luigi is actually hiding in the club. Frankie is finally recaptured as he leaves the club taking Arthur as a hostage but, in an unexpected twist, Arthur is also arrested for harbouring an escaped convict. Ray and Dave are also bundled into the police van to be taken in for questioning. The closing aerial shot of the police convoy taking them away is brilliant.

Printed in the United Kingdom
by Lightning Source UK Ltd.
98950UKS00001B/317-318